Long-Term Care Insurance *NOW!*

An Industry Insider Reveals

Scott A. Olson, CLTC

ISBN 978-1-63784-787-9 (paperback)
ISBN 978-1-63784-788-6 (digital)

Copyright © 2024 by Scott A. Olson, CLTC

All rights reserved. No part of this publication may be reproduced, distributed, or transmitted in any form or by any means, including photocopying, recording, or other electronic or mechanical methods without the prior written permission of the publisher. For permission requests, solicit the publisher via the address below.

Hawes & Jenkins Publishing
16427 N Scottsdale Road Suite 410
Scottsdale, AZ 85254
www.hawesjenkins.com

Cover designed by Carolyn E. Olson

The information in this book is NOT to be considered personalized advice. The content is not intended to provide investment, tax, legal, financial, or any other professional advice. Financial decisions should not be implemented based solely on the contents of this book. Do not act without consulting a licensed investment, tax, insurance, and/or legal professional to help you make decisions based on your unique circumstances.

Visit my website at www.LTCShop.com

Printed in the United States of America

To my wife, my partner, my lover.
words fail me…

Acknowledgments

<u>To Bill:</u>
There are very few people you meet in life who can help you grow in your profession, speak into your life on a spiritual level, and, at the same time, make you laugh so hard your cheeks hurt. Bill Comfort is that man in my life. You are a once-in-a-lifetime friend. Thank you for all the insights and knowledge you've shared with me over the past 25 years. In a not-so-roundabout way, you helped write this book.

<u>To Hersh:</u>
Thank you for the opportunity you gave me. I learned so much from you in such a short time.

<u>To Rex:</u>
In those formative years of my career, you demonstrated, in word and deed, what a true insurance professional is. Thank you.

Contents

Acknowledgments v

Chapter 1
First Things First 1
   Why I Wrote This Book 1
   Long-term care insurance is unfamiliar 1
   Why I am qualified to author a book on this subject 4
   Do NOT buy long-term care insurance if. 4
   How much does long-term care insurance cost? 7
   Important terms and abbreviations used in this book 8

Chapter 2
The Realities of Caregiving 13
   My (first) caregiving story: lessons in what NOT to do 13
   My 2nd time as a caregiver: lessons in what TO DO 27
   My wife's story: the 28 hats of a caregiver 33

Chapter 3
How to Self-insure for Long-Term Care 41
   Why is an insurance agent teaching you
      how to self-insure? 41
   The term "self-insure" 42
   Plans to self-insure for long-term care usually fail 42
   The hidden costs of self-insuring 44
   Two unanswerable questions that make self-insuring risky ... 55
   Self-insuring: the three WORST ways 58
   Self-insuring: a BETTER way 65
   Self-insuring: the BEST way (for some) 66

  Why not "Half-Insure"? 70
  Sophisticated investors and options traders, read this!..........71

Chapter 4
 The State of the LTCi Industry 73
  Why have so many companies stopped selling
   Traditional LTCi 73
  Rate Increases! Rate Increases! Rate Increases! 77
  Claims! Claims! Claims! 88
  Complaints! Complaints! Complaints! 92
  BANKRUPTCIES! BANKRUPTCIES!
   BANKRUPTCIES! 93

Chapter 5
 Long-Term Care Insurance NOW! 97
  4 questions you MUST ask when comparing policies 97
  Traditional Long-Term Care Insurance 100
  Long-Term Care Partnership Policies 102
  Recovery Policies 103
  Hybrid Life Insurance with some kind of a rider 105
  #1 reason most people should NOT buy a Life/
   LTC hybrid 109
  5 reasons someone SHOULD buy a Life/LTC hybrid 110
  Annuity with some kind of a rider 111
  What are the advantages and disadvantages of each
   type of policy? 116
  Sometimes 2 policies are better than 1 120

Chapter 6
 Hybrids! Hybrids! Hybrids! 121
  "Local long-term care insurance specialist" 125
  Use-it-or-lose-it is NOT a flaw; it's a feature 130
  Some hybrids can turn into
   NOTHING! NOTHING! NOTHING! 131
  If you need life insurance, do NOT buy a hybrid. 132
  What makes a "hybrid" good or "not-so-good" 133

Chapter 7

Shopping for Long-Term Care Coverage 135
    Your health history is THE MOST
        CRITICAL FACTOR 135
    How to compare "hybrids" with traditional LTCi 139
    Is a "cash indemnity" policy better or a
        "reimbursement" policy? 148
    Is a monthly benefit better than a daily benefit? 150
    Is a calendar day elimination period better than
        a service day? 152
    Understanding Comdex rankings 154
    7 K.E.Y. questions 155

Chapter 8

What has Washington State wrought? 159
    What is the WA Cares Fund? 159
    What Washington state did right (& wrong) 160
    2 ways the WA Cares Fund and private LTCi are
        nearly identical 161
    6 ways the WA Cares Fund is better than private
        long-term care insurance 162
    9 Ways Private Long-Term Care Insurance is
        BETTER than the WA Cares Fund 164

Chapter 1
First Things First

Why I Wrote This Book

I authored this book for three reasons:

1. Long-term care insurance is unfamiliar to most.
2. Most insurance agents, even most financial planners, know little about long-term care insurance.
3. Most of the newest information on the internet about long-term care insurance is wrong.

LONG-TERM CARE INSURANCE IS UNFAMILIAR

Half-truth: "Long-term care insurance is complicated."

The other half-of-the-truth: "It is complicated because it is **<u>unfamiliar</u>**."

Even though modern long-term care insurance has existed since 1997, most people are unfamiliar with long-term care insurance. ***No one is experienced in shopping for long-term care insurance.***

You've probably bought dozens of auto insurance policies and a few homeowner's insurance policies over the years. You might have bought medical insurance every year and/or a few life insurance policies.

You've probably never shopped for long-term care insurance. Long-term care insurance is usually a once-in-a-lifetime purchase.

No one is familiar with it.

I'm writing this book to help you become familiar with long-term care insurance so that you can decide if it is right for you. And if it is right for you, hopefully, this book will help guide you to the type of policy that may suit you best.

MOST FINANCIAL ADVISORS KNOW LITTLE ABOUT LONG-TERM CARE INSURANCE

Recently, I got a call from a woman who lives in Illinois. She asked, "Are there any long-term care insurance policies available for sale in my state?" I answered, "Yes, of course there are. Ten different companies sell long-term care insurance in Illinois."

She continued, "A relative of mine had a long-term care insurance policy, and it worked well when she needed care. She could afford a beautiful, assisted living facility and lived there for many years. I want the same type of policy for myself. I want the most amount of long-term care coverage for the lowest possible premium."

Then she said this: "I asked my financial advisor, and he gave me a quote to buy life insurance with some kind of a rider. I don't want life insurance. I want straight long-term care insurance. But my advisor said it's no longer available."

> "…my financial advisor said it's no longer available."
> "…my financial advisor said it's no longer available."
> "…my financial advisor said it's no longer available."

I was stunned!

At best, what the financial advisor told her is a half-truth.

It would have been more accurate if the advisor had said: "Straight long-term care insurance policies are available for sale today. However, the companies I represent do not offer them."

That would have been the whole truth.

I'm not saying that the advisor lied to her. He was either lying or just misinformed. Since I believe the best about people, I believe he was just misinformed.

I'm writing this book so that YOU can be INFORMED, even if your financial advisor is not informed.

MOST OF WHAT YOU READ ON THE INTERNET ABOUT LTCI IS WRONG!

It's been six years since I wrote my first book on long-term care insurance. Much has changed about long-term care insurance in the past six years, and a lot has stayed the same. One of the biggest changes is that most of the newest information on the internet about long-term care insurance is wrong.

I will repeat that. It should shock you.

*One of the biggest changes over the past six years is that most of the latest information on the internet about long-term care insurance **is wrong.***

There used to be a lot of reputable websites that informed and educated consumers about long-term care insurance. Now, many of those websites are simply paid advertisements for Big Insurance.

Every week, I will read 5 to 10 new articles about long-term care, long-term care planning, and long-term care insurance. Usually, 80% to 90% of the statements about long-term care insurance are half-truths or, even worse, complete falsehoods. Again, I do not think the writers are intentionally misinforming their readers. They are perpetuating half-truths, and they do not even know it.

In this book, I will endeavor to give you the "other half of the truth" so that you can make an informed decision about long-term care insurance for yourself and your loved ones.

Why I am qualified to author a book on this subject

Since 1995, I have helped thousands of consumers shop and compare long-term care insurance policies. I am licensed to sell long-term care insurance in all 50 states and the District of Columbia. I have taken all the training each state requires to be qualified to sell long-term care insurance. I am an independent insurance agent. I do not work for any specific insurance company.

I was one of the first insurance agents in the country to earn the Certification in Long-Term Care (CLTC) designation. I passed that exam in 1999. I was one of the first insurance professionals to be asked to participate on the CLTC Board of Advisors.

My most important qualification, however, is being a caregiver. I have had family members who needed care but did not own long-term care insurance. I have had family members who needed care who owned long-term care insurance, and they used it. I have seen how these policies work from beginning to end. That helps me do a better job of designing policies for my clients.

Do NOT buy long-term care insurance if…

There are no definitive guidelines for who should buy long-term care insurance. However, there are clear guidelines for those who should NOT buy long-term care insurance.

50% of retirees should NOT buy long-term care insurance (probably)

Why? Because they could qualify for Medicaid-funded long-term care. If someone can easily qualify for Medicaid-funded long-term care, then they should NOT buy long-term care insurance.

Example 1:

If someone is single and retired and has income under $50,000 per year and net worth under $100,000

…he/she should probably NOT buy long-term care insurance because it would be pretty easy to qualify for Medicaid-funded long-term care.

However, it might make sense to buy an inexpensive "recovery" policy, which could help pay for six to twelve months of care. A small, affordable "recovery policy" might help avoid the long waiting lists that are often experienced by those who rely solely on Medicaid to fund their long-term care.

"Recovery Policies" are discussed in Chapter 5.

Example 2:

If someone is married and retired and has household income under $50,000 per year and household net worth under $200,000

…that couple should probably NOT buy long-term care insurance because it would be pretty easy to qualify for Medicaid-funded long-term care.

However, it might make sense to buy an inexpensive "recovery" policy, which could help pay for six to twelve months of care. A small, affordable "recovery policy" might help avoid the long waiting lists that are often experienced by those who rely solely on Medicaid to fund their long-term care.

If they cannot afford a "recovery policy" for both spouses, they should probably buy a "recovery" policy for the spouse who has the most income in his/her name. They should also contact their county's "Agency on Aging" to speak with one of their insurance counselors for advice.

Example 3:

If someone is not yet able to retire

...he/she should probably NOT consider buying long-term care insurance unless he/she has ALL OF THESE higher financial priorities taken care of:

1. Excellent medical insurance (including maximizing contributions to any Health Savings Account or Flexible Spending Account).
2. Long-term DISABILITY insurance to replace at least 50% of pre-tax income if no longer able to work.
3. Enough term life insurance to replace income to support dependents.
4. All high-interest debt paid off.
5. Six to twelve months' worth of living expenses in a savings account.
6. Maximizing contributions to retirement accounts every year.

If all of those priorities are being taken care of, THEN consider buying long-term care insurance.

Lastly, if you live in a state that is considering implementing a payroll tax to fund a government-run long-term care program AND if you earn above average income, you may want to buy a small "starter" long-term care insurance policy.

How much does long-term care insurance cost?

I hear this all the time: "I requested a quote for long-term care insurance from an insurance website. When the agent called me, he wouldn't give me any quotes unless my husband and I first listened to his 90-minute Zoom presentation. We both work full-time and don't have that kind of time just to get a quote."

Your time is valuable. At this stage in your life, it might not make sense to own long-term care insurance. Before you spend a lot of time researching long-term care insurance, you should be able to quickly and easily get a rough idea of what a policy might cost and how much it could cover.

I created an easy solution:

The "Policy Finder" on LTCShop.com

Using a proprietary algorithm I developed, I will pinpoint one or two, maybe three, of the policies that will probably be best suited for you. We'll email you some quotes within one business day.

Here's the best part:

>You do NOT have to provide your name.
>You do NOT have to provide a phone number.
>You do NOT have to speak with an insurance agent.

All you need to do is answer some basic questions and one of my licensed associates or I will email you the customized quote. After receiving your quote, if you'd like to learn more, you can go to our online calendar and reserve a 15-minute introductory call to discuss it in more detail.

Just go to www.LTCShop.com and, using the menu in the top right-hand corner, click on Policy Finder. You can do this on your desktop, tablet, or smartphone.

Important terms and abbreviations used in this book

LTC means "Long-Term Care"

LTCi means "Long-Term Care insurance"

ADLs means "Activities of Daily Living"

There are six ADLs: bathing, dressing, eating, toileting, transferring (from bed or chair), and maintaining continence.

Long-term care means care that assists someone with any of the ADLs or cares for someone who has a cognitive impairment. This care could be "hands-on" assistance or "stand-by" assistance.

Although long-term care is provided in many different settings, most long-term care is provided at home, not in facilities.

Most long-term care is provided by family members, friends, and other loved ones.

Long-term care expenses or **long-term care costs** refer to the costs incurred to pay someone to assist you (or your loved one) with the ADLs.

Long-term care coverage means all the different types of insurance policies that can be used to help pay for long-term care:

1. traditional long-term care insurance,
2. long-term care partnership policies,
3. recovery policies,
4. life insurance policies with some type of a rider, and
5. annuities with some type of a rider.

When I use the term **long-term care insurance,** I am referring to traditional long-term care insurance or long-term care partnership policies *ONLY*.

Long-term care partnership policies are just like traditional long-term care insurance, except there is one additional benefit: a long-term care partnership policy can protect your assets from Medicaid, even if the long-term care partnership policy runs out of benefits.

Partnership policy and **LTC Partnership policy** are shorthand for Long-Term Care Partnership Policy.

Long-term care partnership programs refer to the legislation enacted in a specific state setting standards for and approving the sale of long-term care partnership policies.

Partnership-Qualified Policy is another name for a long-term care partnership policy. If a policy meets all the requirements of a state's long-term care partnership program, the policy is considered to be Partnership-Qualified.

Public long-term care insurance refers to a government program funded by taxes, created to help pay for long-term care expenses. The Washington Long-Term Care Trust Act (aka, "WA Cares Fund") is one example.

Private long-term care insurance means insurance policies issued by insurance companies, not the government. Although not run by the government, private long-term care insurance is highly regulated by each state's government as well as the federal government.

Hybrid means a policy that combines life insurance with some sort of rider that may allow the life insurance benefits to be used by the insured to pay for long-term care expenses. "*Life/LTC*" is a common shorthand for this type of policy.

Hybrid can also mean a policy that combines a deferred annuity with some sort of rider that may allow the annuity to be used by the insured to pay for long-term care expenses. "***Annuity/LTC***" is a common shorthand for this type of policy.

Hybrids are often referred to as **asset-based long-term care** because they usually have a cash value or a death benefit. Traditional long-term care insurance does NOT have any type of cash value or death benefit (with a few exceptions).

Stand-alone long-term care insurance is another way of describing traditional long-term care insurance and long-term care partnership policies. "Stand-alone" is used to emphasize that these policies are not paired with any type of life insurance.

Daily Benefit means the maximum amount the policy can pay for each day the insured receives care. Daily Benefit is synonymous with **Daily Maximum** and **Maximum Daily Benefit** and **Daily Cap**.

Monthly Benefit means the maximum amount the policy can pay for each month the insured receives care. Monthly Benefit is synonymous with **Monthly Maximum** and **Maximum Monthly Benefit** and **Monthly Cap**.

A policy with a $200 Daily Benefit is comparable to a policy with a $6,000 Monthly Benefit because $200 x 30 days = $6,000 per month.

Lifetime Benefit means the maximum amount the policy can pay in benefits over the lifetime of the insured. Lifetime Benefit is synonymous with **Lifetime Maximum, Maximum Lifetime Benefit, Lifetime Cap, Policy Limit, Pool of Money, Total Benefit, Benefit Amount, and LTC Benefit Amount.**

Shared Care is offered in some policies, which allows married couples or domestic partners to share each other's Lifetime Benefits. Shared Care is synonymous with **Shared Benefit, Shared Maximum,** or **Shared Pool**.

Inflation Benefit is how the Daily (or Monthly) Benefit and the Lifetime Benefit increase over time so that the benefits try to keep pace with the increasing cost of care. Inflation Benefit is synonymous with **Inflation Protection**.

Elimination Period is similar to a deductible. It's the number of days of care for which the policy will NOT pay any benefits.

Chapter 2
The Realities of Caregiving

My (first) caregiving story: lessons in what NOT to do

Thanksgiving Day, 1996.

I was 31 and a newly licensed insurance agent with John Hancock in Tampa, Florida. I drove my wife and 5-year-old son from Florida to New Jersey to spend the holiday with my in-laws. While there, I asked my father-in-law if he had any long-term care insurance. He said, "What's that?" I gave him a brief introduction to the subject. He replied gruffly, "That's never gonna happen to me."

Conversation.
Over.

Seventeen months later, in April 1998, we got "The Call". I remember it vividly. I had just put on my suit and tie and was about to go to the office when the phone rang. My wife answered. It was her sister. Her father had come home from work the day before and had a stroke while eating at the dining room table.

My father-in-law spent a week in the hospital until he was stable. He was then transferred to a skilled nursing facility. He had intensive speech therapy and physical therapy in hopes of a full recovery. Sadly, there was no improvement. He was completely paralyzed on his left side. He couldn't do anything for himself. He needed help bathing, dressing, getting in and out of bed, and on and off the toilet.

Medicare (and his Medicare supplement) covered the full cost for 60 days in the skilled nursing facility. Medicare stopped paying on day 61 because his level of care was downgraded from "skilled care" to "custodial care."

Medicare does not pay any benefits when care is only "custodial."

"Custodial care" is also called "personal care." Personal care includes assistance with bathing, dressing, toileting, getting in and out of bed, etc. Medicare primarily only pays for rehabilitative care like speech therapy, physical therapy, respiratory therapy, etc.

MedicAID pays for "personal care," but only if your income and assets are low enough to qualify. My in-laws had too much in savings to qualify for Medicaid.

The nursing home administrator had a meeting with my mother-in-law and asked her how she planned to pay for her husband's care going forward. She asked, "How much will it cost?" Stunned by the administrator's answer, my mother-in-law replied, "For that price, I'll take him home and care for him myself."

So.
She.
Thought.

She lived in New Jersey. She had three daughters. The youngest, my wife, lived in Florida. Another daughter lived in Massachusetts and worked full-time as a teacher. The other daughter lived about 15 minutes away. She was a business owner, and she had to run her business.

My mother-in-law was half-right. There were some things she could do for her husband:

- She could cook for him.
- She could feed him.
- She could give him his medications.

But her husband, the love of her life, was dead weight. She could not move him even though he was only 5'2" and 110 pounds. She couldn't get him out of bed. She couldn't get him into the shower. She couldn't get him on and off the toilet. She couldn't roll him over.

She had no choice but to have a hospital bed placed in their bedroom, and she hired a live-in home health aide to care for him.

My mother-in-law's life, as she had known it, was over.

When a loved one's health has been compromised, the stress can be unbearable, especially when it's a spouse. But she also had the stress of hiring (and living with) a stranger to care for him. And there was the financial stress. He could not work anymore, and she had to withdraw from their savings and retirement accounts every week to pay the home health aide. She also had her own health problems to deal with: arthritis, insulin-dependent diabetes, and heart disease.

The cost for the live-in home health aide was less than that of a nursing home in New Jersey, but not much less. Since nursing homes in Florida were cheaper than in New Jersey, my mother-in-law decided it would be best to move her husband and herself to Florida.

So.
She.
Thought.

She put her house up for sale and temporarily moved her husband into an assisted living facility in New Jersey. She packed up their things and sold the home they'd lived in for 40 years. My wife and I found a beautiful, brand-new assisted-living facility just outside of Tampa.

It was just a few miles from my home, and the price was reasonable. My father-in-law was wheeled onto an air ambulance at Teterboro airport in New Jersey and flown to a private airfield in Tampa, adjacent to the Tampa Bay Buccaneers practice field. My mother-in-law and her husband settled into the new assisted living facility for what she expected would be the remainder of their lives.

So.
She.
Thought.

Unfortunately, their time at the assisted living facility didn't last long. My mother-in-law loved her husband deeply. They were always very affectionate to each other. That affection never subsided, even when he was bedridden. Her deep love for him caused her to put a lot of stress on herself to make his life better. She was always trying to make him feel more comfortable. This strained her relationship with the aides who worked in the assisted living facility. When her husband needed something, she would request an aide and get upset if an aide didn't show up immediately.

But she also needed a break from him. Due to the stroke's effect on his brain, he would yell in his sleep. She would get up to comfort him every time he yelled. She couldn't get a good night's sleep. It was just too much for her.

So, she moved my father-in-law to a brand-new skilled nursing facility about 10 minutes from my home. And my mother-in-law moved into the spare bedroom in my 1,600-square-foot home. She would live with us while her husband lived out the remainder of his life in the skilled nursing facility.

So.
She.
Thought.

This new plan didn't last very long either. My mother-in-law couldn't stand being apart from her husband. Visiting him every day in the nursing home was better than not seeing him. But who wants to spend all day in a nursing home?

At this point, it made more sense for all of us to live together and hire home health aides to care for him. We couldn't all fit into my 1,600-square-foot house, so my mother-in-law bought a 2,500-square-foot house with four bedrooms. She and her husband could each have their own bedroom, and she would be able to get a good night's sleep.

These moves occurred over only 18 months.

That's right. Over a period of 18 months, he was moved SIX times. He lived in two different skilled nursing facilities, two different assisted living facilities, and two different houses. All these changes were tough on him. But it was even tougher on his wife and his daughters (and me).

You could say that all these moves in such a brief period resulted from poor planning. The truth is, <u>there was no planning</u>. Remember what he told me that Thanksgiving: "That's never gonna happen to me."

There's no need to plan for something that's "never gonna happen."

It would have been a lot easier on his wife and daughters if they had discussed these issues as a family in advance and made some plans, just in case. But they didn't.

Moving my wife and son into the same house with my mother-in-law and father-in-law was a difficult decision. It was something my wife wanted. How could I say no to her? It was something my mother-in-law wanted. How could I say no to her? And how could I say no to my father-in-law? He was disabled and suffering and needed care.

Please understand. I am sure I had a choice. But it didn't feel like I had a choice.

Besides, this new living arrangement would be fine, right? After all, my mother-in-law was going to hire home health aides to take care of her husband every day.

So.
I.
Thought.

The plan was to have a home health aide there 12 hours per day, seven days per week, from 8am to 8pm. The home health aide would take care of all his needs: bathe him, dress him, prepare his meals, do his laundry, assist him with toileting, and get him in and out of his bed, his wheelchair, and his recliner. It was a physically taxing job since he couldn't do anything for himself (other than feed himself). Every day, he would be transferred 10 to 12 times. (A transfer is moving someone to and from their bed, toilet, wheelchair, recliner, etc…) Every aide we had was a saint. Unfortunately, my mother-in-law didn't always treat them like saints. She was often rude to them. Sometimes, she was downright mean to them.

Needless to say, the aides would quit. Home health aides have a tough job, and like everyone else, they want to be appreciated for the work they do. For the first few months, we had constant turnover. One aide might last a week. Another aide might last two weeks. They never gave notice. They just wouldn't show up. I woke every day worrying, "Will the home health aide show up today?"

When you hire a home care agency, they often have a large pool of aides to draw from. You may not get the same aide every day, but at least you will have someone there every day. However, home care agencies cost more than independent aides. My mother-in-law did not want to pay what the agencies were charging. That is why she would only hire independent aides. Her retirement accounts were dwindling, and she needed to keep expenses as low as possible.

When a home health aide did not show up, guess who became the home health aide for the day?

Me.

I was already the nighttime home health aide. Each night, I would give my father-in-law his medication, change his adult brief a couple of times, and roll him over throughout the night so he would not get bed sores. When an aide was a "no show" in the morning, I became the daytime caregiver, too, because neither my wife nor my mother-in-law was physically able to transfer him.

I had to do it.

No one else could do it.

What choice did I have?

What else could I do?

The impact on my career and my income was severe. I had to miss a lot of work and eventually lost my job and all my benefits. In a short period of time, I had no more savings.

But what was I to do?

My in-laws needed my help.

Eventually, we found two home health aides who were WONDERFUL. One worked four days per week and the other three days per week. They each worked from 8am to 8pm. I was able to work full-time again during the day, and I did my usual caregiving duties at night. Thankfully, my mother-in-law started showing the aides appreciation and kindness.

This lasted about six months. Then, my mother-in-law disagreed with one of the aides, and that aide quit. Shortly after that, the other aide quit. My mother-in-law asked me to "fill in" until she found replacements. I told her she needed to call a home care agency. I couldn't be the substitute home health aide anymore. I had to earn a living and support my wife (her daughter) and my son (her grandson).

Needless to say, she was upset with me. Within a few weeks, she had her husband in the same air ambulance that flew him to Florida, and they flew back to New Jersey. They moved into an assisted-living facility near their hometown, but the assisted-living facility did not accept Medicaid. As they began to run out of money, they both had to move into a nursing home that accepted Medicaid. They both passed away in that nursing home.

My father-in-law's decision not to plan for long-term care had devastating consequences that affected his wife, his daughters, his son-in-law (me), and his grandson (my son).

Shortly after my in-laws passed away, my wife and I divorced.

THE LESSON: Everyone needs to sit down with their loved ones and make a plan for long-term care. Your plan may (or may not) include some long-term care insurance.

Long-term care insurance is NOT the plan. Long-term care insurance can help fund the plan.

LONG-TERM CARE INSURANCE NOW!

Either way, everyone needs a plan for long-term care.

THE FROG IN THE POT—BEWARE OF "CAREGIVING CREEP"

We have all heard the story about the frog in the pot of water. If a frog is put in boiling water, he will jump out right away to protect himself. However, if you place a frog in a pot of room-temperature water and slowly turn up the heat until it reaches a boil, the frog won't notice the subtle differences, and he will eventually die.

I do not know if that story is true or not, but the message is applicable to being a caregiver:

Caregiving responsibilities often creep up unexpectedly.

If my mother-in-law had called me after her husband had a stroke and said:

> "Scott, I want to move to Florida and buy a house for all of us to live in, and I want you to be my husband's nighttime caregiver. You may also need to be his caregiver during the daytime, possibly a few days a week, if the home health aides don't show up. You'll probably lose your job and burn through all your savings, and it might even ruin your marriage. How's that sound?"

Obviously, I would have said, "NO! I am not doing that."

But that is what happened. It started off with a little bit, then a little bit more, then a little bit more, until finally, as a caregiver, I was in a prison from which I felt like I had no way out.

My story is not unique. Caregiving responsibilities creep up on the caregiver and may eventually overwhelm the caregiver.

THE 5 TYPES OF STRESS CAREGIVERS FACE EVERY DAY

> *"Mom, you don't need that long-term care insurance. You took care of me growing up. The least I can do is take care of you when you grow old."*

I hear this a lot. Adult children have good intentions and mean what they say, but they often don't really know all that is involved with caregiving. Usually, in their mind, "taking care of my parents as they grow old" means bringing them groceries, taking them to the doctor, managing their medications, etc. Those tasks are the ***easiest*** part of caregiving.

I have never heard anyone say, "I will help my parents with grocery shopping, doctor appointments, and medication management, AND I will also help them with bathing, dressing, and toileting every day."

The stress of caregiving is difficult to imagine. Having experienced it twice, I have some insights I can share. Below is a summary of the five types of stress caregivers face every day:

1. physical stress
2. emotional stress
3. mental stress
4. financial stress and
5. family stress

PHYSICAL STRESS

For someone who has never been a caregiver, physical stress is the easiest stress to understand. I'm a father. I helped take care of my son when he was a baby and a toddler. And I've been a caregiver to a grown man.

Helping a toddler get in and out of the tub is much easier than helping a grown man get in and out, and helping a toddler on and off the toilet is much easier than helping a grown man get on and off the toilet.

Caregiving can be very strenuous!

It often requires a lot of lifting.

In my mid-thirties, in great shape, I could transfer a 5'2, 110lb man from his bed to his wheelchair and back again. But it was hard! He was paralyzed on his left side. He was dead weight. It was even harder to get him on and off the toilet. If it was that hard when I was in great shape in my 30s, why would someone think they can take care of their spouse when they are both in their 70s or 80s?

Caregiving is physically hard.

Try this:

Tell your loved one to lie down on the bed. Try to get them out of bed without their assistance. Or have your loved one sit in a chair and try to move them from that chair to another chair without their assistance. Now, do that 10 times a day. That is the physical stress of caregiving.

EMOTIONAL STRESS

I have been a caregiver twice, both times for an in-law. I have never been a caregiver for anyone who raised me, and that has saved me from a lot of the emotional stress of caregiving.

Seeing a loved one's health decline brings on a lot of emotional stress. But there is the added emotional stress of changing roles. The child becomes the parent. Having long-term care insurance does not remove the emotional stress you experience when you see your loved one's health declining. However, the emotional stress is lessened when you only have to *manage* your loved one's care and not provide all of the hands-on care. The hands-on care brings with it even more emotional stress.

The emotional stress of caregiving is hard enough when there has been a healthy relationship between the parent and the adult child. How much greater is the emotional stress for an adult child who was raised in a dysfunctional family or is taking care of an abusive parent?

MENTAL STRESS—THE STRESS OF THE UNKNOWN

This is the hardest stress to explain to someone who has never been a caregiver.

The mental stress comes in the form of anxious questions:

- When will the next health crisis hit?
- When will he/she need more care?
- When will this be over? (which is immediately followed by guilt)

As a caregiver, in the back of your mind, you are always on alert. You are responsible for your loved one's safety. You do not know when they might fall, faint, or have trouble swallowing their food. Their health is already bad, but you do not know when their health may suddenly get worse.

In those few minutes when things are less stressful, and you have a moment to reflect, your mind wanders, and you think, "How long will this last? How long will he need care?" Then, after asking yourself, "When will this be over?" you are flooded with guilt.

When you raise a child, there are milestones. Your child gradually becomes more and more independent, and you can anticipate when those milestones are likely to be reached: feeding himself, potty training, personal hygiene, dressing himself, not wetting the bed at night, etc...

When caring for an aging loved one, it's just the opposite. The aging loved one becomes more dependent on you. The amount of care required increases.

And there's no end date.

There's no way of knowing how much longer your loved one will need care. There are no mile markers. The future is unknown and that is why it is so stressful. In my opinion, this is the most stressful part of being a caregiver and this is what makes caring for an aging loved one ***1,000 times harder than raising a child.***

FINANCIAL STRESS

The financial stress from caregiving can come in many different forms.

The first time I was a caregiver, I missed a lot of work. My income plummeted. I eventually lost my job and my benefits due to inconsistent performance. I used up all my savings to pay my bills. There was A LOT of financial stress.

But, my mother-in-law also had a lot of financial stress. She and her husband worked hard for years. They scrimped and saved. They had a nice retirement nest egg. But after her husband's stroke, he couldn't work anymore. She had to write big checks every week to the home health aides. Eventually, she spent every penny they'd ever saved, including all the equity in their home.

The financial benefits of long-term care insurance are clear. Even a small policy would have made a big difference for my (first) mother-in-law.

My (second) mother-in-law received almost $300,000 in benefits from her long-term care insurance policy. Her policy relieved nearly all of the financial stress associated with her care.

Family Stress (sibling, spouse, etc....)

When a loved one needs care, the responsibilities of caregiving are rarely divided evenly amongst family members. This can lead to strife and bitterness between family members. Caregiving rarely brings families together. **Caregiving often pulls families apart.**

A few years ago, my mother kept falling in her home. She needed to move into an assisted-living facility. She lives in New Jersey. I live thousands of miles away. My sister lives in New Jersey, but she is physically disabled and unable to help. All of the caregiving responsibilities fell to my brother. Other than offering advice and lending a caring ear, I have done nothing to help my brother take care of my mother. My brother had to do it all. For example:

- He helped her downsize (she had a lot of stuff)
- He put her house on the market
- He moved her from New Brunswick, NJ, to Cape May, NJ, so that she would be near him
- He handled all her financial, insurance, tax, and legal matters
- He handled all her healthcare matters and doctors' appointments
- He did her grocery shopping for her and managed her medications
- He took her to her doctors' appointments

As if that wasn't enough, he had to do all of this shortly after his wife was diagnosed with a very aggressive form of cancer. His wife died about a year after the diagnosis.

He was caring for his wife, parenting two teenagers, working a full-time job, and taking care of our mother's affairs, all at the same time. **Caregiving responsibilities never come at a convenient time, and they are rarely divided evenly between siblings.**

My 2nd time as a caregiver: lessons in what TO DO

It was March, 2017. My (new) wife and I were on our way to Jacksonville, Florida, for the long-term care insurance industry's annual convention. When our plane landed, my wife received an ominous text message from her brother. "Call me when you can." She called him as soon as we got into the rental car. My (new) mother-in-law was slurring her speech, and she had to go to the emergency room. After tests, the doctors concluded she'd had a series of small brain bleeds caused by CAA, cerebral amyloid angiopathy. The neurologist described it as "potholes" in the brain.

The next day, my wife was on a plane to Redlands, California, to be with her mom. Only ten months earlier, we'd moved from Redlands to Camano Island, Washington. When we moved, my wife promised her mother that she'd be there for her whenever she needed her. We did not expect that time would come so soon.

After a few days, her mom was released from the hospital and went home. She was mildly cognitively impaired. She had some balance issues. She was not able to safely shower by herself. She was not able to safely dress herself. She needed someone to help her.

My wife's father had his own health issues. He had a bad hip. He had some lingering paralysis from a stroke he'd had a few years earlier. He'd had a heart valve replacement. He was not physically able to help his wife in the shower or help her get dressed and undressed.

Fortunately, eleven years earlier, my mother-in-law had purchased a long-term care insurance policy.

My wife found the policy in the filing cabinet and called a leading home care agency, Amada Senior Care. They took care of everything. They arranged for home health aides to be there every morning to help with bathing, dressing, and breakfast. **Amada even took care of**

all the paperwork to file the claim with the long-term care insurance company.

Due to my father-in-law's uncertain health, we all decided that he and my mother-in-law should move to an assisted-living facility near us in the state of Washington. They spent a month and a half sorting through decades of memories. Then my brother-in-law and I drove a U-Haul to Washington containing their most treasured possessions.

Shortly after moving into the assisted-living facility, my father-in-law passed away in his sleep. We were all in shock. One of the first questions my mother-in-law asked was, "Am I going to have to leave this beautiful place?" She asked that question because she knew she would lose some of his pension income and part of their social security income. Thankfully, we knew that between the pension income, social security, her rental property income, and her long-term care policy, she would never run out of money. She would be able to stay there for as long as she lived. We assured her of that.

My mother-in-law settled into a relatively comfortable routine at the assisted-living facility. It wasn't perfect, but she was safe. The facility was beautiful and clean. It had wide, carpeted hallways. There was a grand piano in the lobby. The food was delicious. We ate there at least once a week. Most importantly, the staff were kind, and she developed friendships with some of the other residents.

We took her to church and out to dinner every week. She was able to see her grandsons, her daughter, and me a few times every week. She attended the weddings of two of her grandsons and even got to travel to California to see her granddaughter get married.

Except for the first 90 days, her long-term care insurance policy covered the full cost of her care in the assisted-living facility. She was a resident there for a little over three years.

And then COVID hit.

The next five months were horrible. I won't tell you all the details. You can read about it in my wife's book, "*Caregiving Reality.*" For my purpose in this book, all you need to know is that the facility told my mother-in-law that if she came to our house to visit us, she would be quarantined for 14 days each time.

For five months, my mother-in-law hadn't been able to have any socialization with her friends in the facility because of COVID. Then, just as the government and corporate restrictions started to loosen, the facility came down hard with this new 14-day quarantine rule.

My mother-in-law was devastated.

My wife was devastated.

When my wife told me about this new quarantine requirement, I knew she wanted to move her mother into our home. I also knew my wife would never ask me if we could move her mother into our home. My wife knew about my first caregiving experience. She knew how hard it was on me and my son. There's no way she would ask me to "go through that again." But she didn't realize that this time would be different for a few reasons.

Transferring is the key

The hardest part about my first caregiving experience was the transferring. Every day required 10 to 12 transfers. This time, there would be no transferring. My mother-in-law was able to transfer herself. She just needed her rollator. A rollator is like a walker with wheels and hand brakes. Whenever she visited us, she would use her rollator to get from the dining room table to the bathroom and back.

So, when my wife told me about the quarantine, I grabbed the rollator and tested it.

- Could she safely get from the spare bedroom to the bathroom?
- Could she safely get into the bathroom and close the door behind her?
- Could she safely get from the spare bedroom to the kitchen?
- Were the turns too sharp?
- Would she hit the edge of the wall, lose her balance and fall?

Once I concluded that she could maneuver safely through our house, I was in favor of her moving in with us. My wife cried happy tears.

However, before my mother-in-law moved in, I insisted that all three of us (my wife, my mother-in-law, and me) come to a few agreements:

1. My mother-in-law could only live with us as long as she could transfer herself (i.e., get in and out of bed by herself, get on and off the toilet by herself, etc.). If she got to the point where she couldn't get herself out of bed or on and off the toilet, she would have to move back into the assisted-living facility.

2. We would agree to live together for five years and no more. If, after five years, she was still alive, she would have to move back to the assisted-living facility.

3. Anyone of us would have the power to veto the arrangement ***at any time***. In other words, at any time, any one of us could say, "No more! We are ending this living arrangement," and my mother-in-law would move back to the assisted-living facility. There would be no judgment and no guilt if one of us chose to exercise the veto power.

Before moving her into our home, we only needed several grab bars installed in her bedroom, hallway, and bathroom. The bathroom also needed to be renovated by replacing the bathtub with a walk-in shower. Unexpectedly, her long-term care insurance policy paid several thousand dollars toward the bathroom renovation and grab bars.

She moved into our home on September 15th, 2020. We were prepared for a living arrangement that we expected would last at least a few years. Sadly, my mother-in-law passed away only eight months later, on May 20th, 2021. My mother-in-law needed care for about four years. Over three years of her care was spent in the assisted-living facility.

Clearly, my second time as a caregiver was a lot different than my first time as a caregiver. Here's how:

Physical stress

There was very little physical stress. My first time as a caregiver, I provided hands-on physical care for several hours every day, seven days per week. During my second time as a caregiver, nearly all of the hands-on caregiving was provided by the aides at the assisted-living facility. When we moved her to our home, most of the hands-on caregiving was provided by the home health aides we hired. My wife did provide some hands-on care on Sundays and sometimes at night. But, being a caregiver one day per week is a lot easier than being a caregiver seven days a week.

Emotional stress

When we moved my mother-in-law into our home, I knew it would be a lot harder, emotionally, on my wife than me. After all, it's her mom. There were some difficult conversations she had to have with her mom and some role-reversal. And it's hard to see your loved one's health decline. There's really nothing that can be done to avoid the emotional stress. You just have to deal with it. However, **it's easier to deal with emotional stress when all the other stresses are at lower levels**. If my wife had to do all the hands-on caregiving, the emotional stress could have been too much to handle.

MENTAL STRESS

When she lived in the assisted-living facility, we knew she was safe. The staff was on-site, 24 hours a day, and they were just a "pull cord away". That helped relieve a lot of the mental stress.

When she moved into our home, much of the mental stress was nipped at the bud because of the agreements we made. At any time, any one of us could "veto" the living arrangement. A lot of mental stress was relieved just having that understanding from the start, knowing that if it got too hard, we could just end it. One reason we were able to make that agreement was because we knew that there would always be enough money for her to go back to the assisted-living facility because of her long-term care insurance policy.

FINANCIAL STRESS

My mother-in-law had an excellent long-term care insurance policy. We didn't have to worry about how her care would be paid for. Also, because we didn't have to provide all of the hands-on care, both my wife and I were still able to work full-time even when her mother was living with us.

FAMILY STRESS

There was very little family stress for many reasons. We all kind of knew who would be responsible for what.

- My wife took the lead in her mother's care and all her financial matters.
- One of her older brothers, who is very handy, lived in the same town where the rental properties were located. He could help maintain the properties and deal with the renters.
- The other older brother lived in Illinois and did as much as he could, in particular, providing a listening ear and loving, compassionate counsel.

All the legal and financial affairs were in order: the trust, the will, the medical power of attorney, and the financial power of attorney.

Her policy was covering the full cost of her care in the assisted-living facility. When we moved her into our home, the policy continued to cover the full cost of the home health aides. My wife and her two brothers didn't have to worry about their mother's financial situation. Family stress and financial stress often go hand-in-hand. Since the policy covered the cost of care, there was no need to worry about the money.

Caregiving can pull families apart. Of course, your loved ones are going to care for you as you age. Long-term care insurance helps your loved ones take care of you even better. Long-term care insurance can help your loved ones be your care managers, NOT your caregivers. Long-term care insurance benefits your loved ones as much as it benefits you.

My wife's story: the 28 hats of a caregiver

In the last section, I wrote:

"Long-term care insurance can help your children be your care managers, NOT your caregivers."

Caregiving is HARD, with or without long-term care insurance.

Long-term care insurance can help relieve *some* of the stresses of caregiving, particularly the physical stress and the financial stress. But there's still a lot that your loved ones will need to do for you.

Even though my wife's mother had a great long-term care insurance policy and most of the hands-on care was provided by the aides, there were still A LOT of responsibilities my wife had to handle for her mom. So, as a tribute to my wife, here are the 28 hats she wore during the four years her mom needed long-term care.

1. she did her mother's grocery shopping
2. she prepared meals that her mother loved
3. she attended all of her mother's medical appointments
4. she managed all of the medications
5. she often cleaned her mother's apartment at the assisted-living facility
6. she loved and encouraged her mother
7. when necessary, she helped her mother with showering, dressing, and toileting (usually no more than once or twice per week).
8. she managed her mother's finances
9. she managed her mother's three rental properties
10. she went with her mother on fun day trips sponsored by the assisted-living facility
11. she taught a Bible study for her mother and friends every week
12. she took her mother to church every weekend
13. she drove her mother everywhere she needed to go
14. she was the point person for all of her mother's medical emergencies
15. she handled everything to do with her mother's stay in the assisted living facility
16. she interviewed, hired, managed, and fired home health aides
17. she filed the long-term care insurance claim each month
18. she kept her brothers updated on their mother's health and finances
19. she filed her mother's federal and state income taxes every year
20. she negotiated the sale of her mother's rental properties
21. she invested the proceeds from the sale of the rental properties
22. she flew with her mother to California to attend the eldest granddaughter's wedding
23. she was the executor of her will
24. she handled all her legal affairs, including two trusts

25. she handled the estate's final tax returns
26. she filed the claim for her father's life insurance death benefit
27. she filed the claim for her mother's life insurance death benefit
28. she disbursed all the assets to the heirs

And she did all that while she was working a FULL-TIME job and taking care of her husband (me), two of our four sons, and two dogs. I cannot even count how many cats there were! ;-)

It would have been impossible for my wife to work full-time if we did not have home health aides. We would not have had the home health aides as much as we did if it were not for my mother-in-law's long-term care insurance policy.

"I WILL JUST KILL MYSELF."

First off, I want to congratulate you for having the guts to read a section entitled, "I will just kill myself."

You are either curious ("Why would Scott entitle this section 'I will just kill myself'") or you are reading this because you have actually said (or thought), "I will just kill myself," whenever the subject of long-term care has come up. This section is for you. Let's discuss it. First, understand this:

Long-term care is <u>NOT</u> end-of-life-care.

Long-term care is living-a-long-life-<u>with</u>-care.

Long-term care is not about extending the lives of those with a terminal illness. Long-term care is about assisting our loved ones, who may have many more years to live. They just need assistance with basic, daily activities (like bathing and dressing).

Hospice care is "end-of-life-care." Hospice care means someone has a terminal illness and they have less than six months to live. People who need assistance with daily tasks are not dying. People who need assistance with daily tasks can often live long, rewarding, fulfilling, and even (dare I say) **happy** lives.

My mother-in-law needed assistance with daily activities (like bathing and dressing) for four years. She was on claim, receiving benefits from her long-term care insurance policy that entire time.

During that period of time, she was able to witness some special moments:

- Her eldest granddaughter got married,
- Two of her grandsons got married,
- One grandson was baptized, and
- She was present when another grandson (following in her footsteps) was sworn into the military. We have a picture of them together at his swearing-in ceremony. (She is holding the crest for the Air Force, her branch, and he is holding the Navy crest.)

She would have missed these moments if she weren't here. But most importantly, from her perspective, her grandchildren would have missed her deeply if she had not been there for those special moments.

She enjoyed everyday things, too:

- She went for walks most days. Using her rollator, she would walk around the facility or walk a few blocks to the drug store to buy her favorite candy.
- She attended a Bible Study (or two) every week.
- She went to church with us every weekend and out to dinner a couple times a week.
- I would take her to see classic movies on the big screen at the local cinema and to KFC (she loved fried chicken).

- The assisted-living facility sponsored outings to local concerts and special restaurants.

Most importantly, she was surrounded by her loving family. Her sister and her sons and her grandchildren would fly from Montana and California and Illinois to visit her. The grandkids would usually stay with her in her two-bedroom, two-bath unit in the assisted-living facility *so they could have more "grammy time."*

Joyce did all these things while she was on-claim receiving benefits from her long-term care insurance policy. That is why I say:

Long-term care is NOT end-of-life-care.

Long-term care is living-a-long-life-<u>with</u>-care.

People who need long-term care are the same people who are the "pre-boards" at the airport.

Joyce was one of those "pre-boards" when she flew to Wisconsin to see her first grandchild get married.

Joyce was one of those "pre-boards" when we flew to Southern California for her husband's memorial service and honor guard.

Joyce was one of those "pre-boards" when she flew to Southern California to see her granddaughter get married.

When someone is "less-abled," it does not mean that they want their life to end. They can still live a rewarding life. They just need extra assistance. Long-term care insurance helps people afford that extra assistance.

Joyce needed care for four years. She received over $280,000 of benefits from her long-term care insurance policy. She was NEVER in a nursing home. Long-term care insurance is NOT "nursing home insurance." **Long-term care insurance is a wonderful way to stay out of a nursing home.**

He told me he would "just opt-out"

A few years back, someone told me that if it came time for him to need long-term care, he would "just opt-out." At first, I was stunned by his statement because he was adamant about it. He did not say, "Maybe I'll kill myself." He was dead earnest (no pun intended) that if he ever needed long-term care, he would end his life. He would "just opt out."

I said:

"OK. It is clear you have made up your mind. What is your plan for your loved ones? If your wife comes to you and says, 'I have been diagnosed with Parkinson's, what will you say to her? Will you hand her a bottle of tranquilizers and a big glass of water? Are you going to tell her to 'just opt-out'?"

I continued:

What if your wife comes to you and says, "My mom has Alzheimer's," what will you do? Will you tell your mother-in-law to go to sleep in the garage while the car is running? Will you tell her she needs to "just opt out?" What if your daughter comes to you and says, "Dad, I've got Multiple Sclerosis." Will you tell her she needs to "just opt out?"

The more I spoke to him, the more riled up I got. So, of course, I continued.

"If you need help bathing and dressing, are you really going to kill yourself? Being disabled does not mean you cannot make a difference in someone's life. Being disabled does not mean you stop loving others or that others stop loving you. The value of your life is not based on your physical abilities (or disabilities) but on the amount of love and joy you experience and share with others. Would you stop loving your family if you became disabled? Would they stop loving you?"

I continued, "My mother-in-law is receiving 'long-term care.' She needs help showering and dressing every day. Should she kill herself because of that? She enjoys the company of her daughter and her grandchildren. Yesterday she went to the symphony. Today, she is getting a massage at her chiropractor's office. This afternoon, she will come to my home and spend time reading by the fire while our cat purrs on her lap. Do you really think she should kill herself because she needs help with bathing and dressing?"

I ended with this:

"Do the responsible thing and make a plan for long-term care. Your plan may not include long-term care insurance, but everyone needs to have a plan."

"Just like we all need to plan for retirement, we all need to plan for long-term care because most of us, at some point in our lives, are going to need some form of long-term care."

I know my response to him was harsh, but I said it with good intentions, hoping it would reach him.

After speaking with him, I thought about it further:

>How does one determine **_when_** to self-terminate?

If you break your hip and need rehab for several months, are you going to self-terminate?

If you have a stroke and are partially paralyzed, are you going to self-terminate? What if you can recover from the stroke?

In both scenarios, you will need care while you rehabilitate.

Usually, by the time you conclude it's time to self-terminate, you are not strong enough or aware enough to get the job done.

Besides all that, have you ever had a loved one attempt suicide? It is very traumatic for the loved ones. I know firsthand.

Chapter 3
How to Self-insure for Long-Term Care

Why is an insurance agent teaching you how to self-insure?

In the next few sections, I will share with you some ideas about how to self-insure for long-term care. You may be wondering why an insurance agent, who sells long-term care insurance, would teach you how to self-insure for long-term care. Here is why. Every day I see this:

- Someone has a change in their health.
- They decide they should buy long-term care insurance.
- They apply for a policy.
- Their application is declined.

Unfortunately, most people have no choice. They are forced to self-insure for long-term care because they are not healthy enough to qualify for a long-term care policy.

Now, I am not talking about someone who gets cancer or someone who has a heart attack. It's pretty easy for someone to purchase long-term care insurance if they have recovered from a heart attack or if they have beaten cancer.

Long-term care insurance companies are NOT concerned about health conditions that can kill you. Think about it.

Long-term care insurance companies ARE concerned about health conditions that will NOT kill you but will affect your ability to function:

- back problems,
- joint problems (especially knee, hip, or shoulder),
- osteoporosis,
- severe asthma,
- diabetic complications, and
- side effects from COVID

These are all examples of health issues that can prevent someone from being able to purchase long-term care insurance.

The term "self-insure"

To all my associates in the insurance industry, I understand that to insure means to transfer risk to another party. I understand that the term "self-insure" is an oxymoron because you cannot transfer risk to yourself. You either transfer the risk or you retain the risk. Retaining 100% of the risk is not insuring. But I'll still use the term "self-insure" for this discussion because most people understand what "self-insure" means.

"Co-insure" is a real thing and can be a very smart way to approach long-term care planning. "Co-insure" means you retain part of the risk, and you transfer part of the risk. We will look at co-insuring later in the book under the section entitled "Why not half-insure?"

Plans to self-insure for long-term care usually fail

A plan to liquidate assets to pay for long-term care expenses often turns into "daughter care" or "spouse care."

Please understand when YOU need care, you will probably not be the one making the big decisions anymore.

Nine times out of ten, your loved ones, who will be responsible for you, will make the big decisions.

Not you.

And your loved ones may have to make these decisions under a lot of stress: emotional stress, financial stress, and family stress. Your loved ones may even have health problems of their own to deal with.

In my experience, when faced with the reality of caring for you, your loved ones are likely to look at the situation one of two ways:

"He probably has less than six months to live. We can take care of him for six months. There is no need to take money out of the retirement accounts. Six months is not that long. We can do it."

OR

"He might need care for many years. He would not want us to liquidate his retirement savings to pay for his care for several years. It is not that hard. We can do it."

That is why I said above:

A plan to liquidate assets to pay for long-term care expenses often turns into "daughter care" or "spouse care."

Since 1995, I have spoken with thousands of people in-person, over the phone, and through the Internet. Below are a few thoughts they have shared about how owning long-term care insurance was one way they hoped to protect their loved ones from taking on the burdens of providing care. These are actual quotes from real people just like you.

"There is a selfish aspect of my thinking. If I need care, I don't want my wife to scrimp (on my care). There should be no reservations about using the insurance coverage instead of spending down assets."

"The best reason I have heard for buying LTC insurance is so your kids don't have to agonize over whether or not to get you the care you need, which might otherwise cost them their inheritance. Who would want to put that trip on his kids?"

"This is about money, but it is also about family consideration. Those who have had parents and had to struggle to take care of them while trying to take care of their own family and work at their jobs know that maintaining an ailing elderly parent can be an incredibly challenging situation mired with guilt, weariness, and financial strain for those who are trying to help. I do not want to put that all on my family."

"Just like life insurance, LTC insurance is not for the person who is insured – that person will get care no matter what. LTCi protects the family and, more importantly, the spouse. Have you ever seen an 85-year-old woman trying to care for an 87-year-old man who can't get himself bathed and dressed? Even if she could care for him, doing this day after day will soon take a toll on her health. Kids can help, but usually only for a limited time."

The hidden costs of self-insuring

Here's a question you need to ask your future self.

"How much income was that asset generating before I had to liquidate it?"

Think about it.

Take a minute to pause and think about it:

> *"How much income was that asset generating before I had to liquidate it to pay for my long-term care expenses?"*

$100,000 of long-term care expenses does <u>NOT</u> reduce your portfolio by $100,000. It reduces your portfolio by much more than that.

$500,000 of long-term care expenses does <u>NOT</u> reduce your portfolio by $500,000. It reduces your portfolio by much, much more than that.

$1,000,000 of long-term care expenses does <u>NOT</u> reduce your portfolio by $1,000,000. It reduces your portfolio by much, much more than that.

How much is your portfolio reduced for every $100,000 of long-term care expenses you incur? The only way to answer that question is to answer the first question:

> *"How much income was that asset generating before I had to liquidate it to pay for my long-term care expenses?"*

Let's dig a little deeper.

How much do you earn, on average, from your investments?

5%?
7%?
8%?
10%?
12%?

On average, the S&P 500 has returned a little over 8% per year over the past 20 years. Let's use 8% as an average annual return on your investments. And, to keep the math easy, let's assume that the cost of care is $100,000 per year. Let's also assume that the cost of care never goes up.

$100,000 of long-term care expenses does NOT reduce your portfolio by $100,000. Liquidating $100,000 of your investments to pay for long-term care reduces your portfolio by $100,000 PLUS the income $100,000 would have generated for you every year for the rest of your life (and your spouse's/partner's life, if applicable).

Let's consider an imaginary couple: Ricky and Lucy. Ricky is 74. Lucy is 69.

Many years ago, Ricky and Lucy decided to self-insure for long-term care because they have a seven-figure retirement nest egg.

On his 75th birthday, Ricky trips over a set of bongo drums, and his back is seriously injured. He will need long-term care for the rest of his life.

Lucy withdraws $100,000 from their retirement savings to pay for his first year of care. The following year, Lucy's investment income will be about $8,000 less than the previous year because she no longer has the $100,000 she withdrew to pay for Ricky's care.

A year later, she withdraws another $100,000 to pay for his second year of care. That year, Lucy's investment income will be about $16,000 less than it used to be. Why? Because she has had to withdraw a total of $200,000 to pay for Ricky's care. Instead of earning 8% on that $200,000, she is earning nothing on that $200,000 because it's gone.

The third year that Ricky needs care, she withdraws another $100,000. That year, her investment income will be about $24,000 less than it used to be because she has had to withdraw $300,000 to pay for Ricky's care. Instead of earning 8% on that $300,000, she is earning nothing on that $300,000 because it is gone.

The fourth year that Ricky needs care, she withdraws another $100,000. That year, her investment income will be about $32,000 less than it used to be because she has had to withdraw a total of $400,000 to pay for Ricky's care. Instead of earning 8% on that $400,000, she is earning nothing on it because it's gone.

The fifth year that Ricky needs care, Lucy withdraws another $100,000. That year, her investment income will be about $40,000 less than it used to be because she has had to withdraw a total of $500,000 to pay for Ricky's care. Instead of earning 8% on that $500,000, she is earning nothing on it.

Ricky dies.

That is good news for Lucy because she was tired of withdrawing $100,000 every year from their retirement savings to pay for his care. The bad news is that Lucy's income will be $40,000 LOWER every year for the rest of her life than it would have been if she hadn't had to liquidate $500,000 to pay for Ricky's care.

That $500,000 is permanently lost. The $40,000 of income she would have earned on that $500,000 every year is permanently lost.

That $500,000 is permanently lost. The $40,000 of income she would have earned on that $500,000 every year is permanently lost.

If Lucy lives ten years longer than Ricky (which is highly likely), the $500,000 in long-term care expenses paid for Ricky's care would have reduced her net worth by $1,020,000 ($500,000 in principal plus $520,000 in lost investment income).

This is the hidden cost of self-insuring. When someone self-insures for long-term care, they lose the asset used to pay for the care and permanently lose the income that the asset was generating for them.

I know a woman who retired in her mid-fifties. She and her husband settled down to enjoy a long, well-deserved retirement. She loved spending time with her dogs and her horse and taking them on long rides along the beautiful nature trails behind her house in north Florida. However, only seven years after retiring, her husband was diagnosed with early-onset Alzheimer's. He was in his early seventies.

What should she do?

Should she liquidate their retirement accounts to pay for his care each month? She was only in her early sixties and counting on the retirement accounts to fund her retirement years for at least two more decades.

Should she give up all the things she loved to do and care for him 24/7 at the expense of her own health?

What should she do?

Fortunately, she had another choice. Several years before he was diagnosed with Alzheimer's, they had purchased long-term care insurance. Over the next 11 years, his policy paid over $970,000 towards the cost of his care, nearly every penny of the cost of his care.

He was able to receive his care at home for all but the last few months of his life. His wife spent those 11 years overseeing his caregivers, not being his caregiver. And she enjoyed her dogs and horse every day, thanks to their decision to insure, not self-insure.

How to Turn $40,000 into ~~$280,000~~ $878,522

My mother-in-law bought her long-term care insurance policy in 2006. Over 11 years, she paid a little less than $40,000 in premiums for her policy. Like most long-term care insurance policies, the premiums stopped once she started to receive benefits from her policy. She was on claim for about four years and received a little more than $280,000 in benefits from her policy before passing away.

Would she have been better off just investing the money instead of paying the premiums to an insurance company?

No.

The $40,000 of premiums, which turned into $280,000 of benefits, increased her net worth by about $878,522. Here's how:

We avoided over $200,000 in capital gains taxes because we did not have to rush to sell her rental properties.

My father-in-law's original plan was to "self-insure" for long-term care. He said, "If we need care, we'll just sell the rental properties." He had owned these properties for decades, and were fully depreciated.

We calculated that if he sold the properties, he would have to pay over $100,000 in federal and state capital gains tax PER PROPERTY.

Because my mother-in-law had an excellent long-term care insurance policy, they did not have to sell the rental properties. Her policy covered nearly the entire cost of her care until she passed away (except for the first 90 days of care).

We diversified her assets.

When her husband died, the basis of their rental properties was "stepped up." That meant we could sell the properties immediately and not have to pay any capital gains taxes. We sold two properties after he died and invested most of the proceeds in dividend-paying stocks. By doing this, she had about 50% of her net worth in real estate and about 50% in dividend-paying stocks. The stock dividends averaged about 5% per year.

We were comfortable investing her money in stocks because she did not need the money to pay for her care. Her long-term care insurance policy was covering the full cost of her care. At the rate she was using the policy's benefits, we had about 5 to 6 years before the policy would run out of benefits. We reasoned that a 5-to-6-year time horizon was long enough to safely invest her money in high-quality stocks, and we could weather most market corrections. We also invested most of her pension and social security income.

She started receiving care at home; then, she moved to an assisted living facility for about three years before moving into our home. While in the assisted living facility, the policy covered the entire cost of her room and board and her care. She did not have to use her pensions, social security, or any of her rental property income. She had a cash flow positive of over $5,000 every month. We invested that extra income into more dividend-paying stocks. Over four years, we invested $312,700 of her income into dividend-paying stocks.

Again, we were only comfortable investing her excess income in stocks because she did not need the money to pay for her care right then. Her long-term care insurance policy was paying for her care.

We planned to sell her last rental property about a year before her long-term care policy ran out of benefits. We would then invest the proceeds in a mix of dividend-paying stocks and investment-grade bonds. The interest from the bonds, the dividends from the stocks, her pensions, and her social security would create enough income to cover the full cost of her care for as long as she might live.

Again, we had a five to six-year time horizon. There were a couple of big market corrections during that time. Since she did not need the money, we did NOT have to withdraw her money when the market was down. Since she did not have to sell her investments to pay for her care, the money we invested grew…substantially. The day after she died, we liquidated the stocks. They had grown from $312,700 to $442,522.

The one rental property she did not sell lost some value when she first moved into the assisted living facility. Fortunately, we did not have to sell it at that time. During the pandemic, it lost a little value again. Overall, it ended up gaining $185,000 from the time she moved into the assisted-living facility until it sold shortly after her death. If we had been forced to sell that property early on, she would have missed that $185,000 gain. Most of this gain occurred in the 12 months before she passed away. Again, we could postpone selling that property because she had guaranteed income from her long-term care insurance policy every month.

We avoided even more capital gains tax by waiting until she passed away to sell her stocks and her last rental property. Since we did not have to sell the last rental property or the stocks before she died, we saved about $51,000 more in federal and state capital gains taxes because of the step-up in cost basis upon her death.

When you add the:
+ capital gains tax savings,
+ dividend income from the stocks,
+ capital appreciation on the stocks and
+ property value increases,
= The $40,000 of long-term care insurance premiums turned into $280,000 of long-term care insurance benefits, increasing her net worth by about $878,522.

What if she had NOT purchased long-term care insurance?

If she had not purchased long-term care insurance, we would have had to liquidate her rental properties early on, pay huge capital gains taxes, and then we would have had to invest the money very conservatively, earning only 1% or 2% interest. She would have ended up on Medicaid if she lived long enough. That was something we did NOT want to do. The Medicaid facilities in our area were HORRIBLE compared to the private-pay facilities. Our goal was for her to have the best care possible; thankfully, that is what she got!

Here's a breakdown:

+ $200,000 saved on capital gains taxes from two smaller rental properties.

+ $312,700 invested from her excess monthly income since her long-term care insurance covered the full cost of her care every month

+ $129,822 earned from stock dividends and appreciation

+ $185,000 increase in value of the largest rental property

+ $51,000 capital gains tax savings by not having to sell any of the stocks or the last rental property until after she passed away, and we received a step-up in cost basis.

= $878,522 increase in net worth

The Gains From Self-Insuring Are Relatively Small

The bigger your investment portfolio, the less there is to gain from "self-insuring."

You probably never had anyone say that before now. I'll repeat it:

> *The bigger your investment portfolio,*
> *the less there is to gain by "self-insuring."*

In other words, the more money you have, the more sense it makes to own long-term care insurance.

Let's look at some examples:

Suppose you can buy one million dollars of long-term care insurance benefits for $6,000 per year. I don't know if you can purchase a million dollars of long-term care insurance for $6,000 per year. The cost of a long-term care insurance policy depends upon many factors, including your:

- age at the time you apply for a policy,
- health history,
- gender, and
- marital status (couples get discounts when they apply together)

LONG-TERM CARE INSURANCE NOW!

Many of my clients buy more than a million dollars of long-term care insurance benefits and pay less than $6,000 annually. But, for the sake of discussion, let's assume that you can buy one million dollars of long-term care insurance benefits for a premium of $6,000 per year.

To simplify the math, let's also assume your investment portfolio is worth $1,000,000. If you choose to self-insure for long-term care and not spend $6,000 for long-term care insurance, your portfolio would only increase by 60 basis points this year. For those unfamiliar with the term, 60 basis points is an easy way to say "six-tenths of 1%" or "0.6%". ($6,000 is 0.6% of $1,000,000).

If you have a $1,000,000 investment portfolio, the upside of self-insuring is only 60 basis points per year. The downside of self-insuring could be several hundred thousand dollars, possibly even a million dollars, for a catastrophic long-term care event.

If you have a $2,000,000 investment portfolio, the upside of self-insuring is only 30 basis points per year. The downside of self-insuring could, again, be several hundred thousand dollars, possibly even exceeding a million dollars or more for a catastrophic long-term care event.

If you have a $3,000,000 investment portfolio, the upside of self-insuring is only 20 basis points per year. The downside of self-insuring could, again, be several hundred thousand dollars or even a million dollars or more for a catastrophic long-term care event.

If you have a $4,000,000 investment portfolio, the upside of self-insuring is only 15 basis points per year. The downside of self-insuring could, again, be several hundred thousand dollars or even a million dollars or more for a catastrophic long-term care event.

This is why I said at the beginning of this chapter:

The bigger your investment portfolio, the less there is to gain by "self-insuring."

Here is another way to look at it:

Would you alter your asset allocation to gain an extra 60 basis points per year if the new asset allocation could result in you losing hundreds of thousands of dollars from your portfolio? The answer is obvious. Of course you would not alter your asset allocation to gain only 60 extra basis points if it would put hundreds of thousands of dollars at risk. That is the exact reason why long-term care insurance makes sense for people with a seven-figure investment portfolio.

And another way:

Wouldn't it make sense to reduce the return on your portfolio by 60 basis points to protect it from potentially losing hundreds of thousands? Again, the answer is obvious. Sacrificing 60 basis points to protect hundreds of thousands of dollars is a no-brainer.

Long-term care insurance is portfolio insurance.

Let me repeat that:

Long-term care insurance is portfolio insurance.

I have been banned from some early retirement forums for daring to make such a heretical statement. So, I'll say it again:

Long-term care insurance is portfolio insurance.

A catastrophic long-term care event is probably the only thing in your life that could cost seven figures (other than your residence). By sacrificing a little bit of your return each year, you can protect your portfolio from what is probably the only catastrophic risk from which you have not yet protected your investments.

There is very little to gain by self-insuring. There is potentially a lot to lose by self-insuring.

Why would anyone choose NOT to protect themselves from what is probably their largest potential loss?

When all emotion is removed from the decision, the choice to own or not own long-term care insurance boils down to fundamental risk management.

It is logical. It just makes sense.

Two unanswerable questions that make self-insuring risky

Can you imagine someone saying this:

"If I take the money, I would normally pay in homeowner's insurance premiums and invest that every year for the next 30 years, and if I can earn on average about 8% per year, and the average house fire or wind damage or lightning damage is only about $78,000 in repairs if something happens in 30 years, I'll have more than enough saved up to pay for the repairs."

I've had hundreds of conversations with people across the country about self-insuring for long-term care. Those who are initially inclined to self-insure usually say something like this:

"If I take the money I would normally pay in premiums and invest that every year from now until about age 80, and if I can earn on average about 8% per year, and the 'average stay' is only 2.8 years, when I need care in my late 80's I'll have more than enough saved up to pay for the average stay."

Why would someone say something like this about long-term care but never say anything like this about other types of insurance?

A house fire, wind damage, or lightning strike can happen at any time.

But in our minds, long-term care is far, far away.

In our minds, the idea of having our health compromised and needing someone to assist us with basic daily activities, like bathing and dressing, is something that is many years into the future.

But the reality is that any one of us could need long-term care as soon as tomorrow. How many people in the emergency room right now woke up this morning thinking, "I'll probably go to the emergency room today?"

My (first) father-in-law had a massive stroke in his seventies. He needed care for seven and a half years, the last few years being in a nursing home. In that same nursing home was a man who also had a stroke. He was 20 years younger than my father-in-law. He had a stroke in his fifties, and he lost most of his speech and cognitive abilities and needed help to walk. How many years do you think he needed care? How did his care needs affect his wife's financial security?

The younger someone is when they need care, the greater the potential loss.

Most plans to "self-insure" for long-term care assume care will be needed very late in life. What if you or your loved one needs care a few years from now? How would that affect everything you have worked for?

Long-term care is NOT end-of-life care.

Long-term care is care needed ***until*** the end of life.

LONG-TERM CARE INSURANCE NOW!

I read about a man who retired at the age of 40. He saved, budgeted, and invested wisely. A few years after his retirement, his wife started growing tumors around her spine. The tumors needed to be surgically removed. The surgery was as dangerous as the tumors themselves. She could end up being partially or completely paralyzed. Unfortunately, he didn't think about long-term care insurance until after her diagnosis. She was not even 50 years old.

The greatest risk is NOT if you or your spouse/partner needs care in the last two minutes of the 4th quarter of your retirement years. The greatest risk (especially to the healthy spouse/partner) is if you need long-term care in the first half of retirement OR, even worse, before you retire. Either of those scenarios could have devastating consequences on the financial independence of the healthy spouse.

The first unanswerable question is:

When will you (and/or your loved one) need long-term care?

The second unanswerable question is:

For how long will you (and/or your loved one) need long-term care?

Most plans to self-insure rely on an "average stay in a nursing home." Nursing home statistics are poor measures of long-term care. According to a study done by the Congressional Budget Office, only about 1 out of 8 people who need long-term care are in nursing homes. Most people who need long-term care receive their care at home. **"Average nursing home" statistics fail to include all the years someone receives care at home before they ever step foot in a nursing home.**

When I look at my parents, both sets of my in-laws, and my stepparent, the "average length of care" is 3.8 years (so far).

- Two died suddenly and did not need any long-term care.

- One has needed care for 3 years and is still receiving care.
- Two needed care for 4 years.
- One needed care for 7.5 years.
- One has needed care for 8.5 years and is still needing care.

Averages mean nothing when you are the one hit by lightning.

Are you the one who will need care for zero years, or eight-plus years, or somewhere in between?

Self-insuring is risky:

1. When will you (and/or your loved one) need long-term care?
2. For how long will you (and/or your loved one) need long-term care?

Since the answers to these two questions are unknowable, most plans (not all, but most plans) to self-insure are simply betting, not planning.

Self-insuring: the three WORST ways

Here is the WORST way to "self-insure for long-term care":

Tell yourself that you are going to self-insure for long-term care.

That's it.

That is the worst way to self-insure. Many people tell themselves (and only themselves) their "plan to self-insure." They never have a meaningful conversation with the people who mean the most to them, those who will be responsible for their care.

LONG-TERM CARE INSURANCE NOW!

Here is something you may not have realized:

> When you need care,
> you will NOT be the one making
> the big decisions anymore.
> (probably)

When your health (and/or cognition) is compromised, and you need help with basic, daily tasks, the people you have invited into your life, your dearest loved ones, will be responsible for your care and safety.

They will be the ones making the big decisions.

If you have never shared your plans to self-insure with them, <u>how do you know they will do it?</u>

Keep in mind:

1. Planning for long-term care is NOT planning for your death.
2. Planning for long-term care is planning for your quality of life (should you ever need daily assistance).
3. Most importantly, planning for long-term care is planning for **your loved ones' quality of life** should you ever need daily assistance.

Long-term care planning is not really about "you." It's about "them" (your loved ones).

The purpose of planning for long-term care is to minimize the negative consequences a long-term care event would have on your loved ones' physical, emotional, and financial well-being.

So, please, for the sake of your loved ones, do not keep "your plan to self-insure" a secret. Sit down with your loved ones, discuss it, agree on the plan, and write it out in detail.

The 2nd WORST way to "self-insure for long-term care" is:

Health Savings Accounts

What is a Health Savings Account? Health Savings Accounts (HSAs) are a special type of savings account that allows you to deposit pre-tax dollars into it (just like a traditional IRA).

The money grows tax-free (just like a traditional IRA).

However, unlike a traditional IRA, when you pull the money out of your HSA, you are NOT taxed on it if you use it to pay for "qualified medical expenses." (e.g., co-payments, deductibles, prescriptions, and long-term care costs, like nursing home care or home healthcare.)

When you use the money for medical expenses (or long-term care expenses), the money is NOT taxed.

That is what's unique about these accounts:

- you pay no taxes on the money you deposit into the HSA,
- you pay no taxes on the growth of the money in the HSA and
- you pay no taxes on the money you take out of the HSA as long as it is used to cover qualified medical or long-term care expenses.

It is a brilliant idea.

However, there are three catches:

To deposit into an HSA, your medical insurance policy must be "HSA-compliant." That means your medical insurance policy must have a high-deductible.

There are limits on how much you can deposit into the HSA. Depending on your age and your policy type, you can only deposit between $4,150 and $9,300 per year. (These figures are adjusted every year for inflation).

Lastly, you cannot deposit into an HSA once you turn 65.

You can withdraw money from your HSA to pay for long-term care expenses tax-free. That is why some people view HSAs as a wonderful way to "self-insure for long-term care." But that is the main reason why HSAs should NOT be used to "self-insure for long-term care."

I had a conversation with a couple a while back. They were in their late thirties. They were aggressive savers, and they would probably retire in their mid-forties. They also considered using an HSA to "self-insure for long-term care." They currently had about $40,000 in their HSA and expected it to grow to about $300,000 by the time they reach their mid-sixties IF they contribute the maximum amount every year and make no withdrawals.

There were a few problems with their plan. $300,000 sounds like a lot now, but 30 to 40 years from now, it probably won't pay for more than a year or so of long-term care. However, the biggest problem with their plan was that they did not know when they might need long-term care. What if one of them needed long-term care in their 50s? Their HSA would cover little at that point, and they would need to sell off investments to pay for the care. Liquidating their retirement savings to pay for one spouse's care could wreak havoc on their early retirement and impact the healthy spouse's long-term financial security.

However, there are three more reasons why they should NOT rely on an HSA to "self-insure for long-term care."

To get an HSA, you must have a "High-Deductible Health Plan" (HDHP). High deductibles are great when you're healthy and have no health problems. But high deductibles are "not-so-great" when you have health problems and need medical care. The purpose of the Health Savings Account is to pay the "high deductible."

I have had an HSA since 1999. Every year, I deposit the maximum amount allowed into my HSA. Today, I have less than $20,000 in my HSA. Why? Because I have an athletic wife and athletic sons (I try to be athletic), and we have needed a half dozen knee surgeries, physical therapy, multiple ear surgeries, nose surgery, oral surgeries, knee braces, special dental appliances, orthodontia, prescription eyeglasses, MRIs, CT scans, sleep studies, etc… You name it! We needed it!

Planning to use an HSA to fund your future long-term care expenses assumes you will not have any significant medical expenses from now until you turn 65. That is unrealistic.

Scott, why did you take the money from the HSA to cover the deductibles? Why didn't you let the money stay in the HSA and pay the deductibles with cash from your regular savings account? Simple:

A $6,000 deductible paid from my HSA costs me only $6,000 because it is pre-tax money.

A $6,000 deductible paid from my regular savings account costs $8,000 because it is after-tax money. I must earn $8,000 and pay the income tax (about $2,000) to net $6,000.

Am I suggesting that someone should not have a Health Savings Account? Absolutely not. HSAs are great. Like I said, I have had one for 25 years. However, they are not a sensible replacement for long-term care insurance and are one of the worst ways to "self-insure for long-term care."

The other two reasons to NOT use an HSA to "self-insure for long-term care" are related to taxes.

First, you can use funds in an HSA to pay your LTCi premiums tax-free. Remember, with an HSA, the money grows tax-free, AND the money can be taken out tax-free when used for medical expenses. The IRS considers long-term care insurance **premiums** to be a valid medical expense.

Age-based limits exist, but you can pay some, or possibly all, of your long-term care insurance premiums with pre-tax dollars from your HSA. (Be sure to discuss this with your tax preparer).

Scott, do you use your HSA to pay your LTCi premium? No. I am self-employed. Self-employed people can usually pay LTCi premiums with pre-tax dollars even if they do not have an HSA. There is a special tax deduction for self-employed people that allows this. It is called the "Self-Employed Health Insurance Deduction." So, I get my tax savings from my LTCi premium because I am self-employed.

The second "tax reason" why you should not plan to use your HSA to "self-insure for long-term care" is that withdrawals from HSAs to pay for long-term care are tax-free, but the actual long-term care expenses are tax-deductible. You are better off using your traditional IRA to pay your long-term care expenses.

Withdrawals from traditional IRAs are taxable.

Long-term care expenses are tax-deductible.

In other words, you can wipe out some (probably most) of the tax owed on the withdrawal from your traditional IRA by deducting the cost of the actual long-term care expenses you incur.

The 3rd WORST way to "self-insure for long-term care" is:

Roth IRA

The Roth IRA is the greatest retirement savings vehicle ever created. Roth IRAs are better than traditional 401(k)s and better than traditional IRAs.

The Roth IRA is the greatest retirement savings vehicle because it has:

- Tax-free growth,
- Tax-free withdrawals (after age 59.5),
- No required minimum distributions and
- It is 100% tax-free to your beneficiaries upon your death.

Taking money out of a Roth IRA to pay for long-term care expenses is a terrible way to use the Roth IRA. The Roth IRA is perfect for supplementing retirement income because it is 100% tax-free. It is also ideal for leaving money to your heirs because it is 100% tax-free.

Since long-term care expenses are tax-deductible, you are better off using your traditional IRA or traditional 401(k) to "self-insure for long-term care." Withdrawals from traditional IRAs and 401(k)s are taxable. But you can erase a good chunk of that tax by deducting the cost of the long-term care expenses under "qualified medical expenses" on Schedule A of Form 1040.

- Withdrawals from your traditional IRA/401(k) *increase* your taxable income.
- Long-term care expenses you incur *reduce* your taxable income.

That is why a traditional IRA/401(k) is one of the better funding sources for anyone who plans to "self-insure for long-term care".

Please note: I am not a tax advisor. Consult your tax advisor to determine the best strategies for your unique tax situation.

Self-insuring: a BETTER way

If you plan to "self-insure for long-term care," to get it right, you must do three things:

1. Decide which asset you will liquidate 1st to pay for your long-term care expenses. As I mentioned, a traditional IRA/401(k) is one of the best funding sources for anyone planning to "self-insure for long-term care".
2. Make a list. Put the 1st asset at the top of the list, then add the rest of your assets in the order that you want them liquidated: 2nd, 3rd, 4th, 5th, 6th, 7th, 8th, 9th, etc. You cannot assume you will need only $200,000 of care or only $250,000 of care. Since you do not know how long you might need care, most, if not all, of your assets could be at risk.
3. Share the list with your loved ones and make sure they understand that you do NOT want them to sacrifice their careers, families, or health to be your caregiver.

That last step is the most important part!

The biggest problem with self-insuring is this: your loved ones do not know how long you will need care. Since your loved ones will not know how long you need care, they might hesitate to withdraw money from your accounts to pay someone to care for you. They will usually try to care for you themselves. This burden falls on women more than men.

The best part about having long-term care insurance for my mother-in-law was that there was no hesitation in getting her the care that she needed. There was no strife between her adult children about how to pay for the care. Everyone knew that she had a long-term care insurance policy and that we should use it right away. And we did. There were no arguments over which assets to liquidate to pay for her care.

Your loved ones need to be aware of your plan and agree with you.

Keep in mind, when making your liquidation list, that you do not know when you may need care or how long you may need care. You cannot assume you will need only $XXX,XXX to pay for your care. Your care may cost $XXX,XXX times 2, or $XXX,XXX times 3, or $XXX,XXX times.

We all expected my (first) father-in-law to die within a year after he had his stroke. He lived seven and a half years after the stroke. We expected his care to cost $XXX,XXX. His care cost $XXX,XXX times 5, which, in his case, was everything they had ever saved. He spent the last two and a half years of his life in a Medicaid-funded nursing home.

A "Long-Term Care decision" awaits most of us.

It is better to make these decisions in agreement with your loved ones rather than by yourself.

It is better to make these decisions sooner, when you have more options, rather than later, when it might be a crisis.

Self-insuring: the BEST way (for some)

Self-insuring is risky because you do not know the answers to the two or three important questions I mentioned earlier:

1. When will you need care?
2. How long will you need care?
3. For Couples: How long will you live after your spouse/partner has needed care and passed away?

Long-term care insurance is valuable because it answers all three of these questions.

<u>When will you need care?</u>

It does not matter. With most policies (not all, but most), 100% of the policy benefits are available to you from the moment you are approved and have paid your first premium. Every dollar you pay for care is one less dollar available to generate income.

<u>How long will you need care?</u>

There are policies with an unlimited amount of benefits. No matter how long you might need care, it will never run out of long-term care benefits. For less premium than an unlimited policy, couples often buy policies to share benefits that last 10, 12, 14, or even 16 years.

For those with more modest assets, a well-designed long-term care partnership policy can protect most, if not all, of your assets, even if your policy runs out of benefits. I discuss LTC Partnership policies in Chapter 5.

<u>For how long will you live after your spouse has needed long-term care and passed away?</u>

This question is crucial for someone who must self-insure. Every dollar used to pay for care is one less dollar available to generate retirement income for the surviving spouse. Your retirement assets canNOT simultaneously provide a stream of income that you will never outlive AND be liquidated to pay for long-term care.

That is one reason why I refer to long-term care insurance as portfolio insurance.

So, what is the BEST way (for some) to self-insure for long-term care?

Asset-based long-term care insurance.

These products provide a lot of leverage and tax-friendly ways to fund future long-term care expenses. There are LOTS of options:

- You can fund these products with cash-value life insurance. In some cases, you can avoid paying tax on the gains in the life insurance.
- You can fund these products with deferred annuities. In some cases, you can avoid paying tax on the gains in the annuity.
- You can fund some of these products with a partial transfer from your traditional IRA or 401(k).

These products can be funded with:

- one single premium or
- annual premiums or
- monthly premiums or
- a single premium in combination with annual premiums

If you choose an annual premium, you can set these products to have premiums that are:

- payable for only 5 years or
- payable only 10 years or
- payable only 15 years or
- payable only 20 years

You have LOTS of choices.

These products can **leverage your assets** to pay for long-term care.

When you self-insure, one dollar of assets pays for one dollar of long-term care expenses.

With asset-based long-term care products, one dollar of assets can potentially pay for two, three, four, or even five dollars of long-term care expenses depending upon when you need care, how you set up the product, and whether you include an inflation benefit.

Since the asset-based products can leverage your assets, we can turn $200,000 into a million dollars of long-term care benefits or more. Some of these asset-based products even have a long-term care benefit with no lifetime max. It will pay long-term care benefits for however long you (and/or your spouse/partner) may need care.

And, if you never need long-term care, your beneficiary will get some/most/all of the asset back (possibly with interest), depending upon how you choose to set the policy up when you apply for it.

You can tell that these products are VERY flexible and offer lots of options. That is one reason they are so popular.

With many of these products, the underwriting is relatively easy; it's just a short telephone interview with a nurse from the insurance company. No blood, urine, or medical records are usually required.

Why is the insurance company willing to do this?

If you need long-term care, the asset you use to fund the product pays for roughly the first two years of care. In other words, the insurance company uses YOUR money to pay for the first two years of care you need. They incur little (or no) risk until you need care for longer than two years.

The insurance company is making money on your money. Some of these asset-based long-term care products pay guaranteed interest rates, but they pay less than what the insurance company can make on their investments.

Cash value life insurance is (usually) a horrible investment

Deferred Annuities are (usually) mediocre investments.

However, these asset-based long-term care products are NOT purchased for investment purposes.

These asset-based long-term care products are purchased to help protect your other investments from potentially catastrophic long-term care expenses.

Why not "Half-Insure"?

"To insure" means to transfer risk.

"Self-insure" is an oxymoron because you cannot transfer risk to yourself.

"Co-insure" means to transfer part of the risk.

For this discussion, let us call "co-insure" "half-insure."

My (first) father-in-law needed long-term care for seven and a half years. After spending all their savings, including all the equity in their home, both he and his wife ended up in a Medicaid-funded facility.

The Medicaid facility had kind, loving staff. But the facility itself was old and cramped. I remember visiting him with my wife and son. He had to share a small room with another patient who enjoyed the television on the highest volume all day. There was only one chair in the room. My son sat on the foot of the bed, my wife sat in the chair, and I stood at his bedside.

After he passed away, I did some calculations. I concluded that he and his wife would not have needed to rely on Medicaid if they had had a long-term care policy that covered only half the cost of their care.

As I explained earlier in this book, the hidden cost of self-insuring is that once an asset is liquidated to pay for care, that asset is no longer available to generate income. Because my (first) in-laws had no long-term care insurance, they had to cover 100% of the expenses from their savings. Every time they pulled money out of their retirement accounts to pay for care, that money could no longer generate income for them. It was gone forever.

If they had had a long-term care policy that covered half the cost of their care, they would have only needed to withdraw half the cost of their care from their savings each month. A "half-insure" LTCi policy would have been enough to keep them out of a Medicaid-funded nursing home and in a nice assisted-living facility for many years.

Sophisticated investors and options traders, read this!

Long-term care insurance is something like a "put option".

As you know, a put option gives the owner the right to sell the underlying stock at a specific price, called the "strike price". If the stock falls below that option's strike price, then the option grows in value and helps hedge against the loss incurred by owning the stock.

A "put" is essentially an insurance policy on a stock (or an index).

When all the emotion is removed from the decision to buy long-term care insurance, whether to purchase or not boils down to basic portfolio risk management.

- Puts mitigate risk. A small premium can reduce the risk of losing a lot of money on a particular stock (or index).
- Long-term care insurance mitigates risk. A small premium can reduce the risk of losing a lot of money paying for long-term care expenses.

Chapter 4
The State of the LTCi Industry

Why have so many companies stopped
selling Traditional LTCi

Half-truth:
"Insurance companies are running away from traditional long-term care insurance. Over 100 companies used to sell traditional long-term care insurance. Today, less than a dozen insurance companies sell traditional long-term care insurance."

Other-half-of-the-truth:
Most companies that stopped selling long-term care insurance stopped selling it around 2002. The number of companies selling long-term care insurance since 2002 has been stable (about 10 to 15 companies at any given time in most states).

The important question is:

"Why did so many companies stop selling long-term care insurance around 2002?"

Four reasons:

1. In December of 2000, the National Association of Insurance Commissioners (NAIC) created a new regulation for long-term care insurance pricing to try to prevent rate increases

on newer long-term care insurance policies. The regulation removed the profit incentive from rate increases. This regulation was named the "Rate Stability Regulation." We discuss this regulation in detail in the very next chapter. It is entitled "Rate Increases! Rate Increases! Rate Increases!" States began to adopt this regulation in late 2001 and 2002. Most insurance companies did NOT like this regulation, so many of them decided to stop selling new long-term care insurance policies shortly after this regulation was adopted.

2. Interest rates dropped after 9/11. Long-term care insurance companies collect premiums and then invest those premiums in safe government and corporate bonds. They collect the interest from the bonds to help pay all future claims. When interest rates dropped after 9/11, many insurance companies determined they could not profitably sell long-term care insurance with low interest rates. That is another reason many insurance companies stopped selling long-term care insurance around 2002.

3. Over the past 30 years, the insurance industry, like most industries, has consolidated to reduce overhead and achieve economies of scale. Many companies selling long-term care insurance merged with or acquired other companies selling long-term care insurance. For example, one long-term care insurance company acquired over 20 other long-term care insurance companies.

4. Many insurance companies are more comfortable with life insurance as a solution to long-term care rather than selling long-term care insurance. That is why, if you ask 20 insurance agents for information on long-term care insurance, 19 will probably give you information on life insurance.

Most companies that stopped selling long-term care insurance around 2002 made that decision for one or more of those four reasons.

LONG-TERM CARE INSURANCE NOW!

Let's add some more perspective:

In the 1980s, over 400 insurance companies sold medical insurance. How many companies sell medical insurance today? In most states, individual consumers have more companies to choose from for long-term care insurance than for medical insurance. The same is true for disability insurance. In most states, more companies are selling long-term care insurance today than disability insurance.

> *Today, the companies that sell long-term care insurance specialize in it. They are making a profit, and they know what they are doing. Most insurance companies used to sell dozens of types of insurance. Now, most insurance companies sell only a few types of insurance. They have had to specialize in a few product lines to reduce overhead and increase profits.*

Some insurance companies have found long-term care insurance to be very profitable. Others have not. It is like any other business. The ones who know how to do it stay in the business; the ones who don't get out.

What do the following numbers have in common?

1879, 1871, 1882, 2006, 1909, 1910, 1845, 1857, 1902, 1848

Those numbers are the years in which the companies that sell long-term care insurance today were founded (listed alphabetically):

Bankers Life & Casualty - founded in 1879
Genworth Life Ins. Co. - founded in 1871
Knights of Columbus - founded in 1882
LifeSecure - founded in 2006
Mutual of Omaha Ins. Co. - founded in 1909
National Guardian Life Ins. Co. - founded in 1910

New York Life Ins. Co. - founded in 1845
Northwestern Mutual - founded in 1857
Thrivent Financial - founded in 1902
UNUM - founded in 1848

The average company selling long-term care insurance today has been in business for over 130 years.

You might ask: "But what happens if my long-term care insurance company decides to get out of the long-term care insurance business?"

Nothing happens. The policy my wife and I bought in 2009 is with an insurance company that stopped selling long-term care insurance in 2010. Long-term care insurance is a contract. A contract is a contract, is a contract. If I fulfill my side of the contract (paying the premium), the insurance company must fulfill its side of the contract and pay the policy benefits to us if one or both of us need long-term care.

Long-term care insurance policies are guaranteed renewable. That means that the insurance company cannot cancel the policy. The policy is guaranteed to be renewed every year as long as the premium is paid on time.

If the insurance company stops selling new LTCi policies, they still must fulfill all their legal obligations for every long-term care insurance policy they have ever sold.

What do the following numbers have in common?

1985, 1974, 2011, 2006, 1987, 2016, 1999, 1999, 1987, 1988

Those numbers are the years in which the companies selling long-term care insurance today started to sell long-term care insurance.

LONG-TERM CARE INSURANCE NOW!

The average insurance company selling long-term care insurance today has been selling long-term care insurance for over 27 years.

Rate Increases! Rate Increases! Rate Increases!

The biggest misunderstanding about long-term care insurance today concerns rate increases.

Here are some facts about long-term care insurance rate increases:

- Your premium canNOT be raised because you get older.
- Your premium canNOT be raised because you reach a certain age.
- Your premium canNOT be raised because your health worsens.
- Your premium canNOT be raised because you move to another state.
- Your premium canNOT be raised because you make a claim.
- Your premium canNOT be raised just to increase the insurance company's profits.
- You canNOT be singled out for a premium increase. Everyone in your state who owns that same type of policy must share any premium increase.
- Any premium increase must be based on current and projected claims for your specific policy type.
- In nearly every state, any premium increase must be reviewed and approved by the insurance regulators in that state.

This is all good news. But you are probably thinking, "Why have so many long-term care insurance policies had rate increases?" That is a good question. The answer: **the actuaries were wrong.**

I explain why on my website. Go to www.LTCShop.com and click on "Rate Increases" in the menu.

The actuaries' big mistake was that they did not realize how much people would love long-term care insurance. The actuaries expected about 5% of policyholders to cancel their policies each year. In reality, less than 1% of policyholders cancel their policies each year. Most people who purchase long-term care insurance hold onto it for life. This caught the actuaries by surprise. Claims ended up being twice as high as the actuaries had projected. And that's why many policies purchased in the late 90s and early 2000s have had rate increases totaling 80% and even higher.

The most important question right now is:

"If I buy a long-term care insurance policy today, will I have big premium increases like the older policies had?"

The answer: *No.*

Keep reading, and I will explain why.

First, here is the bad news:

Any long-term care insurance policy purchased today in your state is the most expensive long-term care insurance policy ever sold by that company in your state.

Second, here is the good news:

Any long-term care insurance policy purchased today in your state is the most expensive long-term care insurance policy ever sold by that company in your state.

Go ahead.
Read it again.
There is no typo.

The bad news is the good news.
The good news is the bad news.

The old (cheaper) policies had big rate increases.

The new (more expensive) policies already include all those rate increases in today's pricing. That is why the new policies cost so much more than the older policies.

Insurance regulators do NOT allow any policy purchased today to use the old pricing assumptions. All policies purchased today must use the most current claims data and the most accurate pricing assumptions available to date.

Any policy purchased today must already include all the prior rate increases.

That means every policy purchased today is much more expensive than LTCi policies sold 20+ years ago.

For example, if the older policy sold by the insurance company cost $2,000 per year for "Z" benefits and that policy had an 80% rate increase, a new policy with "Z" benefits must be priced at $3,600 per year or more.

Here is how that is calculated:

$2,000 (older policy pricing)

plus 80% (older policy rate increase)

= $3,600 (new policy pricing)

(To all my actuary friends, this equation oversimplifies how new pricing works, but I am just trying to help consumers understand a complex calculation.)

As a consumer, you may think: "So what, Scott? So what if today's policies include all the prior rate increases? If I buy a policy today, is the premium guaranteed to remain the same for life?"

No. If you buy a policy today, you could still have a rate increase if the insurance company's claims on the new policies are much higher than they have projected.

However, 41 states have enacted strict pricing regulations to help curb rate increases. It is called the "**Rate Stability Regulation**." This regulation helps protect consumers who buy long-term care insurance today.

If your state has passed the "Rate Stability Regulation," these new rules ONLY apply to policies purchased *after* the Rate Stability Regulation became effective in your state.

UNDER THE _OLD_ RULES

When a rate increase was requested, the insurance company could price normal profit levels into the rate increase. In many cases, a rate increase resulted in increased profits for the insurance company.

UNDER THE _NEW_ RULES

If an insurance company requests a rate increase, it must ***decrease*** the profit levels to a cap predetermined by the regulation. Even the rate increase cannot include normal profits, just a small amount to cover administrative costs. Essentially, this regulation removed the profit incentive from rate increases.

UNDER THE _OLD_ RULES

The initial pricing capped profits, but more profit could be made when a rate increase was requested.

UNDER THE *NEW* RULES

Higher profits are allowed in the initial pricing, but the higher profits can ONLY be kept IF THEY KEEP PREMIUMS LEVEL.

UNDER THE *OLD* RULES

The insurance companies were NOT allowed to include any "margin for error" in their initial pricing. There was no cushion in the policy if the claims exceeded the original projections.

UNDER THE *NEW* RULES

Every insurance company is REQUIRED to include a "cushion" in their pricing, which is a margin for error. The goal of the "cushion" is to try to avoid the need for any future premium increases.

UNDER THE *OLD* RULES

The insurance companies did NOT have to certify the accuracy of their pricing assumptions. If their assumptions turned out to be wrong, they would request a rate increase.

UNDER THE *NEW* RULES

Insurance companies are required to have a qualified actuary who certifies that no premium increases are anticipated over the life of the policy. This is why they are required to include a "margin for error" in their pricing.

Please note that the new rules ONLY apply to policies purchased after the Rate Stability Regulation became effective in your state.

Going back to the earlier example, if the older policy sold by the insurance company cost $2,000 per year for "Z" benefits, and that policy had an 80% rate increase, a new policy, under the Rate Stability

Regulation, with "Z" benefits must be priced around $4,032 per year or even more.

Here is how that is calculated:

$2,000 (older policy pricing)
plus 80% (older policy rate increase)
plus ~12% (pricing cushion/margin for error)
= $4,032 (new policy pricing)

That is why I wrote earlier, "Any long-term care insurance policy purchased today, in your state, is the most expensive long-term care insurance policy ever sold by that company in your state."

That's bad news, but it's also good news.

When was the Rate Stability Regulation enacted?

The National Association of Insurance Commissioners (NAIC) created the "model" for the Rate Stability Regulation in December 2000, but it did not become effective in any states at that time. Before the regulation took effect, each state had to pass the regulation. Idaho was the first state to pass the Rate Stability Regulation. The regulation took effect in Idaho on July 1st, 2001. Oklahoma was next to pass the regulation on November 1st, 2001. Seven more states passed the regulation in 2002, nine more in 2003, five more in 2004, three more in 2005, five more in 2006, two in 2007, three in 2008, three in 2009, two in 2010, and finally, New Hampshire was the last state to pass the regulation. It became effective in New Hampshire on June 25th, 2012.

Is the Rate Stability Regulation effective in my state?

Go to LTCshop.com and click on "Rate Increases" in the menu. It will take you to a map showing which states have passed the regulation and which have not.

Is the policy I purchased covered under the Rate Stability Regulation?

Go to LTCShop.com and click on "Rate Increases" in the menu. Click on the state where you were a resident when you purchased your policy. After clicking on the state, you will see the date the Rate Stability Regulation became effective in that state. If your policy was purchased *before* that date, it probably **is NOT** protected by the Rate Stability Regulation. If your policy was purchased *after* that date, it probably **is** protected by the Rate Stability Regulation.

What if I buy a policy in a state with the Rate Stability Regulation, but then I move to a state that does not have the Rate Stability Regulation?

That is OK. You are still protected. Whether or not the Rate Stability Regulation protects your policy is determined by the state you resided in when you purchased your policy, not the state you may move to.

Are some LTCi policies NOT covered by the Rate Stability Regulation?

Yes. Many group policies (e.g., the Federal Long-Term Care Insurance Program, CalPERS, and other self-funded groups) are not required to comply with the Rate Stability Regulation.

Is the Rate Stability Regulation working?

Yes, it is.

Why is the Rate Stability Regulation working?

It works because it uses the old-fashioned carrot-and-stick method to get things done.

The regulation rewards the insurance company with higher profits if they keep premiums level. (That's the carrot.)

The regulation punishes the insurance company by forcing them to lower their profits if they request a rate increase. (That's the stick.)

How effective is the Rate Stability Regulation? Aren't policyholders still getting rate increases?

Many of the rate increases that you hear about are rate increases on policies that are NOT under the Rate Stability Regulation. To determine how well the Rate Stability Regulation works, you must look at the rate increase history of policies sold AFTER the Rate Stability Regulation took effect in your state. Newer policies have had either no rate increases, smaller rate increases, and/or fewer rate increases.

When you apply for a traditional long-term care insurance policy in most states, you must complete a "Personal Worksheet." The "Personal Worksheet" shows the history of the rate increase of the insurance company in the past 10 years (or longer). When you look over the list, you'll see that newer policies have had either no rate increases or smaller rate increases than older policies. That's because the newer a policy is, the more conservatively priced it is.

Be aware of scary headlines about LTCi rate increases.

The following appeared in a respected "newspaper" (website) in 2018:

"…analysts tallied more than 4,500 rate-increase requests nationwide from 2009 to early 2017 by 16 once-big sellers of long-term-care insurance."

This is a perfect example of a "half-truth".

4,500 rate increases sounds scary.
Scary statistics drive clicks.
Clicks generate ad revenue for the website.

LONG-TERM CARE INSURANCE NOW!

Which statement would generate more clicks:

"The 16 largest sellers of long-term care insurance had 4,500 rate increases over past 9 years."

OR

"Average long-term care insurance policyholder had less than one rate increase over the past 9 years."

Both statements are true.

The article failed to include some key facts:

When an insurance company requests a rate increase, they do not request a rate increase for every long-term care insurance policy they ever sold. They only request a rate increase on a particular "policy form" experiencing higher claims projections than initially anticipated.

A "policy form" is like a make and model of a car. Every year, car companies come out with new models. Every year or so, long-term care insurance companies also develop "new models."

If a "policy form" needs a rate increase, the rate increase must be requested in each state plus the District of Columbia. In other words, one policy form that needs a rate increase results in 51 separate rate increase requests.

For example, suppose an insurance company created a "policy form" in 2003, and they called it LTC-2003-TQ. Suppose they sold that policy form from 2003 to 2005, and in 2015, they need to request a 35% rate increase due to higher-than-expected claims. They would have to file 51 separate rate increase requests: one for each state plus one for the District of Columbia.

Breaking down the 4,500 rate increase requests mentioned in the article:

4,500 rate increases mean 88.23 rate increase requests in each state.

(4,500 divided by 51 = 88.23)

88.23 rate increase requests by 16 different insurance companies means about 6 rate increase requests by each insurance company in each state.

(88.23 divided by 16 = 5.5, rounded up to 6)

In the early 2000s, most long-term care insurance companies created at least one new policy form every year. Over 10 years, most long-term care insurance companies would create *at least* 10 policy forms.

6 rate increase requests out of 10 different policy forms mean that about 60% of the policyholders had a rate increase, and about 40% had no rate increase.

Half-truth: "The 16 largest sellers of long-term care insurance had 4,500 rate increases over the past 9 years."

The other half-of-the-truth: "Most long-term care insurance policyholders had one rate increase between 2009 and 2017, and some LTCi policyholders had no rate increases during that same period."

BE AWARE OF THE 2 TYPES OF INFLATION PROTECTION AND HOW ONE TYPE CAN INCREASE YOUR PREMIUM YEARLY.

There are two types of Inflation Benefit:

1. The benefit increases each year do NOT make the premium go up each year.

2. The benefit increases each year DO make the premium go up each year.

These two types of inflation benefits are often confused because the wording in the brochures can be remarkably similar.

Here is an example of language sometimes used to describe "Type A": "Your Daily Benefit will automatically increase by 5% compound every year."

Here is an example of language sometimes used to describe "Type B": "Every year, you will be offered the opportunity to buy additional coverage. Your Daily Benefit will increase by 5% compounded annually."

It is a subtle difference. <u>Buying additional coverage means your premium will go up.</u>

Recently, I was helping a couple shop for long-term care insurance. They were given a quote for a long-term care policy by an insurance agent from whom they had purchased life insurance.

The policies had the same monthly benefit and the same lifetime benefit. The only difference between my quote and the life insurance agent's quote was the Inflation Benefit. The life insurance agent represented a company selling a long-term care policy with a "Type B" Inflation Benefit. Each year, their premium would go up as their benefits went up.

My quote, on the other hand, had a "Type A" Inflation Benefit. The 5% increase in the benefits each year would not make the premium go up each year.

They assumed their life insurance agent had found them the best deal because the quote was lower. After I explained the difference to them, they calculated the future premium increases and realized they would be better off with the "Type A" Inflation Benefit policy.

Know what you are buying. Make sure you understand how the Inflation Benefit can impact the premium.

Claims! Claims! Claims!

Every day, I receive calls and emails from people who want to buy long-term care insurance. I often ask them, "What prompted you to look into long-term care insurance?" One of the most common answers I hear is, "My aunt had a policy, and it helped her get great care for the last several years of her life." Or "My father needed care, and we wouldn't have been able to keep him at home if it wasn't for his long-term care insurance policy."

Every year, hundreds of thousands of people receive benefits from their long-term care insurance policies, and their loved ones see how effective the policies are and want to buy a policy, too.

Many people do not know that long-term care insurance claims data is public information.

According to the NAIC Long-Term Care Experience Report, as of December 2021, the long-term care insurance industry has paid over $190 BILLION in long-term care insurance claims to over 1.5 MILLION policyholders.

https://www.ltcshop.com/naic-long-term-care-insurance-experience-report/

(See page 6, two columns: "incurred claims" and "number of claims open." Look at the "Total Inception-to-Date" rows under individual and group policies.)

Contrary to what you'll often read on the internet, for modern long-term care insurance policies (especially those purchased since 1997), **it is difficult for an insurance company to deny a long-term care insurance claim.**

Every long-term care insurance policy that meets the federal guidelines has an **Incontestability Clause**. According to the clause, an insurer has limited rights to deny a claim or rescind a long-term care insurance policy.

There are three parts to the clause depending on how long the policy has been effective:

1. Suppose the policy has been in effect for six months or less. In that case, the insurance company only needs to show that the insured misrepresented a fact that was material to the coverage's approval. In other words, if the applicant had a health issue not disclosed on the application but otherwise would have caused the application to be declined, then the claim can be denied and/or the policy rescinded.

2. Suppose the policy has been in effect for at least six months but less than two years. In that case, the insurance company must show that the insured misrepresented a fact that was material to the policy being issued AND is related to the medical condition that resulted in the insured needing care.

3. Once a policy has been in effect for two years or more, "it is not contestable upon the grounds of misrepresentation alone." The "policy may be contested only upon a showing that the insured knowingly and intentionally misrepresented relevant facts relating to the insured's health."

NAIC Long-Term Care Insurance Model Act, Section 7 C

That does not mean that filing a long-term care insurance claim is easy.

Several factors can make long-term care insurance claims hard to process for most of us.

> ➤ No prior experience.

The hardest part about a long-term care insurance claim is that it's brand new for everyone. Even though over 1.5 million people have received benefits from their long-term care insurance policies, most of us have never filed a long-term care insurance claim. Even your doctor has lots of experience filing medical insurance claims but little or no experience filing long-term care insurance claims.

> ➤ Medical records delays.

Before approving a claim, the insurance company needs to review the policyholder's medical records. Privacy laws designed to protect us created roadblocks to keep our medical records from getting into the wrong hands. These same roadblocks, however, can cause long delays in getting your medical records from your doctor's office to the insurance company's claims personnel.

> ➤ Legal documents.

The policyholder is usually not the one submitting the claim. If a relative of the policyholder is submitting the claim, the doctor's office needs to know the loved one has the legal authority to represent the policyholder. Until the doctor's office is satisfied that you have legal authority to represent the policyholder, they can't send any records to the insurance company. **That's why legal documents like a durable power of attorney should be in place well in advance.**

> ➤ "Snail mail."

Communication must be HIPAA-compliant. For most companies, communication must be done via "snail mail" or over the phone.

Sending protected health information via unsecured fax or email is a potential HIPAA violation, subjecting the insurance company to huge fines. Having to be HIPAA-compliant can increase delays and frustration for the claimant's family.

➢ Potential Delays.

Lastly, insurance laws in many states require the insurance company to either approve or deny the claim within 60 days of receiving the claim form. The claim is rejected if medical records are not received within that time. The claim can be reopened once all the information has been received. Regardless, this can be very frustrating for the loved one handling the claim.

Fortunately, I used one trick to make the long-term care insurance claims process super easy.

When it was time to file a claim on my mother-in-law's long-term care policy, I did NOT handle her claim. Even though I have been a licensed insurance agent specializing in long-term care insurance since 1995, I did not handle her claim.

We contacted one of the national home care agencies, and they handled it for us. Many national home care agencies process thousands of long-term care insurance claims every year. We had to sign a couple of HIPAA forms, and they took care of the rest.

They handled the claim for free.

It makes sense. The home care agencies get paid by the long-term care insurance companies. They have a financial incentive to set up a system to process long-term care insurance claims successfully.

When you go to the doctor, do you file the claim with your medical insurance company? No. Your doctor's office has a "claims specialist," and the "claims specialist" handles the claim for you.

That is why we had an LTCi claims specialist handle my mother-in-law's claim instead of trying to file the claim ourselves.

Complaints! Complaints! Complaints!

How bad is the service provided by long-term care insurance companies?

To encourage great customer service and to help improve transparency around the quality of service, the NAIC created a Complaint Index. This index compares companies to each other to determine which companies have a better track record for good service.

There are a lot of "consumer websites" where anyone can post anything they want about any insurance company. Interestingly, even companies with a "not-so-good" NAIC complaint index have a surprisingly small number of complaints.

For example, one company has a "not-so-good" NAIC complaint index of 3.5 for long-term care insurance. That complaint index means that the company's complaints from their long-term care insurance policyholders are more than THREE TIMES worse than the average long-term care insurance company.

That particular insurance company has about 130,000 long-term care insurance policyholders. How many consumer complaints do you think were filed against that company to warrant such a high complaint index? 1,000 complaints? 2,000 complaints? 3,000 complaints?

55.

In one year, a company with about 130,000 long-term care insurance policyholders had 55 complaints filed against them. That is one complaint for every 2,363 policyholders.

That same company had about 6,000 long-term care insurance claims approved that year. If all 55 complaints were about claims, then less than 1% of claimants filed a complaint.

Major improvements were made to the long-term care insurance industry in 1993, 1996, 2000, and 2005. However, these changes were usually not retroactive. In other words, if someone bought a long-term care insurance policy in 1991, that policy probably did NOT get the 1993, 1996, 2000, and 2005 improvements (upgrades).

Many complaints about long-term care insurance are about older policies that have not received any upgrades enacted over the years.

I recently spoke with a woman who told me she would never buy long-term care insurance. I asked her why. She said, "My father had a policy, and it would only pay for care in a nursing home. We wanted to keep him at home, and it would not pay for that." I replied, "I bet he bought his policy before 1993." She said, "How did you know that? He bought it in 1989." I explained to her that most policies issued before 1993 were nursing-home-only and would only pay for care received in a nursing home. His policy did not get the "home care" upgrades created in the industry in 1993 and 1997.

BANKRUPTCIES! BANKRUPTCIES! BANKRUPTCIES!

Insurance companies cannot declare bankruptcy. If an insurance company cannot meet its obligations, it is taken into receivership and declared insolvent. A trustee is put in charge of managing the assets and paying the remaining claims.

According to the 2022 annual report by the NAIC, 171 companies have sold long-term care insurance. (click the link and scroll to the bottom half of page 4) https://www.ltcshop.com/naic-long-term-care-insurance-experience-report/

Out of those 171 companies, only 6 of them became insolvent. They were all small companies with below-average financial ratings. Those 6 companies made up about 2% of the long-term care insurance market.

The top seller of these smaller companies was Penn Treaty. Penn Treaty went insolvent. Many factors contributed to their financial woes. One important factor was that they ignored industry standards and sold policies that did not meet the federal guidelines for long-term care insurance. You can learn more about that here:

https://www.ltcshop.com/2016/12/09/yugo-failed-long-term-care-insurance-dead/

For future reference, you can find all Insurance company insolvencies here:

https://www.nolhga.com/factsandfigures/main.cfm/location/insolvencies

Half-truth: Even big insurance companies like AIG can go bankrupt.

In 2008, when AIG needed a bailout, it was NOT the AIG insurance companies that were insolvent. There was a division of the AIG holding company called "AIG-FP." That division sold unregulated "credit default swaps" on subprime mortgage bonds. When the housing market collapsed, "AIG-FP" had to pay billions of dollars to the banks that had purchased the "credit default swaps." **"AIG-FP" needed the bailout, NOT the AIG insurance companies.**

AIG ended up selling some of its insurance companies (which were all very profitable) to pay back all the "bailout money" to the U.S.

Treasury. The U.S. Treasury made a profit of about $22 billion on the deal.

http://www.cnbc.com/id/100397698

Chapter 5
Long-Term Care Insurance NOW!

4 questions you MUST ask when comparing policies

1) How much can the policy pay each day I receive care *at home*?
2) How much can the policy pay each day I receive care *in a facility*?
3) What is the most the policy can pay in benefits over my lifetime?
4) Will these amounts grow each year? If so,
   a. Is the growth guaranteed?
   b. If the growth is guaranteed, what will the benefit amounts be in 5 years, 15 years, or 25 years?
   c. Does the growth in benefits ever stop?
   d. Does the growth in the benefits each year make the premium go up each year?

<u>Questions 1 & 2:</u>

How much can the policy pay each day I receive care at home?

and

How much can the policy pay each day I receive care in a facility?

These two questions highlight the most important part of every long-term care policy: the Daily Benefit. The Daily Benefit is the single most important feature when comparing policies. Why? Because there is a SIGNIFICANT difference between a policy that will pay $300 per day and a policy that will pay only $50 per day.

This is especially important if you buy a policy through your employer. I have seen a lot of "employer-sponsored" long-term care policies that pay only $50 per day. In most states, $50 would not even pay for two hours of home care.

Some policies use a "Monthly Benefit" instead of a "Daily Benefit." Divide the "Monthly Benefit" by 30 to better understand how it compares to a policy with a "Daily benefit".

Question 3:

What is the most the policy can pay in benefits over my lifetime?

The most a policy can pay in benefits over a lifetime is called the "Lifetime Benefit," "Lifetime Maximum Benefit," "Policy Limit," or "Pool of Benefits." A policy with a Lifetime Benefit of $1,000,000 differs greatly from a policy with a Lifetime Benefit of only $50,000.

There is a myth that long-term care insurance policies only pay benefits for two or three years. That is false. It depends upon what you choose to buy. The higher the "Lifetime Benefit" or "Policy Limit," the longer your policy can pay benefits.

Question 4:

Will these amounts grow each year?

Inflation! It affects the cost of everything. I became licensed to sell long-term care insurance in 1995. Back then, most clients bought policies with a daily benefit of about $80. Care today costs a lot more than $80 per day. Fortunately, most of my clients bought inflation protection back then, so their Daily Benefit has grown every year. A policy that does not grow each year will be worth less every year.

Imagine buying a policy in 1995 with an $80 Daily benefit and no inflation protection. That $80 would not buy much care today.

Is the growth guaranteed? There are some policies where the Daily Benefit *might* grow. The illustration will show possible growth, but the growth is *not guaranteed*. I'm not a fan of policies like that.

Planning for long-term care is too important to find out years later that you bought a lemon. There are no "do-overs".

Make sure you buy a policy where you know exactly what it will pay in the future.

What will the benefit amounts be in 5, 15, or 25 years if the growth is guaranteed?
Hopefully, you'll never need long-term care. But if you do, hopefully, it will be many, many, many years in the future. The policy illustration should show you exactly how much your policy benefits will be every year! I include an illustration showing the guaranteed growth with each policy I sell. Knowing how much benefit you will have access to 5, 15, 25, even 35 years from now is essential.

Does the growth in benefits ever stop?
Some policies have inflation protection that stops at some point in the future. The policy benefits stop growing after a certain number of years. There's nothing inherently wrong with that, but it's important to be aware of the difference. When comparing policies, be mindful that one policy may have benefits that stop growing after a certain number of years, and another policy may have benefits that never stop growing.

Does the growth in the benefits make the premium go up?
This is vitally important. Some policies have inflation protection that causes the premium to go up every time the benefits increase. There's nothing inherently wrong with this type of inflation protection.

When comparing policies, it's vital to be aware of this difference. When comparing policies, make sure that the inflation protection riders in each policy are similar (apples-to-apples comparison).

There are 5 types of policies. Which type is right for you?

5 types of policies can help pay for long-term care expenses. All 5 types of policies are similar in that they can help cover the costs of care you receive at home, in an assisted living facility, or a nursing home. Comparing the different types of policies can be confusing. But if you focus on the 4 questions I outlined in the previous section, it will be easier for you to compare policies.

The 5 types of policies are:

1. Traditional Long-Term Care Insurance
2. Long-Term Care Partnership policies
3. Recovery policies
4. Hybrid Life Insurance with some type of rider
    a. LTC benefits are unknown (worst)
    b. LTC benefits are equal to the death benefit
    c. LTC benefits are greater than the death benefits (best)
5. Annuity with some type of rider
    a. Waiver of surrender charge for nursing home care (worst)
    b. Immediate annuity
    c. Immediate annuity that doubles income when LTC is needed
    d. Deferred income annuity (or QLAC - Qualified Longevity Annuity Contract)
    e. Multiplying the premium deposit for LTC benefits (best)

Traditional Long-Term Care Insurance

Traditional long-term care insurance is the oldest and most common form of long-term care insurance. Of the 7,111,139 long-term care policies in-force (as of December 2021), 6,311,826 are traditional long-term care insurance policies.

https://www.ahip.org/documents/AHIP_LTC_State_Data_Report.pdf

Shortly after the creation of Medicare in the late 1960s, companies began offering the very first long-term care insurance policies. Those policies were strictly "Nursing Home" policies. By the early 1990s, with the addition of home care benefits, the policies started to look a little more like the modern policies of today.

In 1993, more improvements to long-term care insurance came with the NAIC Model Regulation of 1993 and the passage of the Health Insurance Portability and Accountability Act of 1996, otherwise known as HIPAA. Most people are unaware that 12 pages of the HIPAA legislation were devoted to establishing consumer protections for long-term care insurance. When insurance companies include these protections in their long-term care policies, the federal government grants the policies "qualified status". "Federally qualified" policies have tax-deductible premiums and, in nearly every case, tax-free benefits.

The last big hurdle for traditional long-term care insurance was the "pricing problem". No one knew how to price it accurately. Therefore, in December 2000, the NAIC created a solution called the "Rate Stability Regulation". **No other type of insurance has this type of pricing regulation.** The regulation removed the profit incentive from LTCi rate increases and created a system of pricing rules that would, over time, result in more stabilized premiums for long-term care insurance.

But none of these changes were retroactive. Each time an improvement was created, it only applied to new policies, not the older policies.

The last major improvement to long-term care insurance occurred in 2005 when President George W. Bush signed the Deficit Reduction

Act. Included in that Act was the expansion of the long-term care partnership programs.

Four states, California, Connecticut, Indiana and New York tested this program in the early 90's. The passage of the Deficit Reduction Act allowed every other state to create similar long-term care partnership programs.

Long-Term Care Partnership Policies

Long-term care partnership policies are just like traditional long-term care insurance, except there is one additional benefit:

A long-term care partnership policy can protect your assets from Medicaid, <u>*even if your policy runs out of benefits.*</u>

For every dollar your long-term care partnership policy pays in claims, you can protect a dollar from Medicaid spend-down and Medicaid estate recovery.

Long-term care partnership policies solve the problem of, "What if my long-term care policy runs out of benefits?" These policies can protect your assets if your policy runs out of benefits.

Long-term care partnership policies answer the question, "How much long-term care insurance should I buy?" **You only need to buy an amount of benefit comparable to the assets you want to protect.**

Long-term care partnership policies are perfect for the middle-class. There's no need to buy a super expensive policy. There's no need to overpay for coverage. Those squarely in the middle-class only need to purchase an amount of long-term care insurance equal to the amount of assets they want to protect from Medicaid.

You can buy more benefits at a higher premium to protect more assets. You can buy less benefits for a lower premium if you have fewer assets. These programs are an equitable and affordable solution for middle-class people who want to ***plan*** for long-term care.

Long-term care partnership policies are the best-kept secret in the insurance industry.

To learn more about these programs, visit my website, LTCShop.com, and click "LTC Partnership" in the menu.

Recovery Policies

In most states, these policies are called "Limited Benefit Convalescent Care." It's not a very appealing name for a policy.

Sometimes, these policies are mislabeled as "short-term care" policies. That can be misleading because some of these policies with inflation protection can pay over $500,000 of benefits for each period of care. That doesn't sound like "short-term" to me. Some states even approve and regulate these policies as traditional long-term care insurance.

For the purpose of this book, I refer to these policies as "Recovery" policies.

First off, there are a lot of these policies out there. And some of them are "not-so-good" compared to others. When comparing these policies, ask these questions:

1) Does the policy use "benefit triggers" similar to long-term care insurance? In other words, do policyholders qualify for benefits if they need assistance with any 2 of the 6 activities of daily living OR have a cognitive impairment and need supervision to stay safe?

2) Does the policy pay benefits for care received in the most common care settings: home care, assisted-living facilities, nursing homes, etc.
3) How much does the policy pay for care at home? **This is VITAL.** Some "Recovery" policies pay much less for care at home compared to what the policy can pay for care in a facility.
4) Does the policy have some inflation protection?
5) Lastly, can the policy be used more than once? Some of these policies have a "restoration of benefits" feature that allows the benefits to be restored if you recover.

Here is an example of the "restoration of benefits":
A client was putting her holiday decorations away in her attic. She stepped backward, missed the ladder, and fell to the floor below. She fractured her pelvis and needed surgery. After a few days in the hospital, she was transferred to a skilled nursing facility to begin physical therapy and the long rehabilitation process. After twenty days in the skilled nursing facility, she was able to go home to continue her rehabilitation. For the next nine months, she had intensive physical therapy at home. At first, she needed a live-in home health aide. As she improved, she cut back on the hours the home health aide was with her. After nine months, she fully recovered and no longer needed assistance.

A "recovery policy" with no elimination period and a $300 daily benefit would have paid $81,000 in benefits during her nine months of recovery. After 180 days without needing care, the policy benefits would be fully restored. In other words, the $81,000 of benefits would be returned to the policy.

In some ways, Recovery policies are better than traditional long-term care insurance:

1) They usually don't have any elimination periods. That means that benefits are payable from the first day you qualify for benefits.

2) Most Recovery policies pay the daily benefit regardless of the actual cost of care. You can use the "extra money" any way that you want to use it.
3) Most pay benefits "in cash," so there is more flexibility in choosing care providers.
4) These policies can pay benefits for care that may only last a few weeks or a couple of months. Most traditional long-term care insurance policies will only pay benefits if your care is expected to last 90 days or longer.
5) Lastly, these policies have noninvasive, "simplified underwriting". In most cases, we can get a Recovery policy approved in 5 business days or less.

Hybrid Life Insurance with some kind of a rider

Hundreds of life insurance policies with some kind of rider can help pay for "long-term care" expenses. Some of these policies might be just fine for life insurance purposes. That doesn't mean it's a good way to plan for long-term care. Since this book focuses on paying for long-term care, I'll teach you how to evaluate these policies based on their long-term care benefits. I've divided these policies into three types, from worst to best: **LTC BENEFITS ARE UNKNOWN (WORST)**

Unknown? Unknown? How could a life insurance policy have unknown benefits? It's true. Many of these policies have long-term care benefits that are ***unknown*** until the time of claim. The most common example of policies like this are indexed universal life insurance policies with a "chronic illness" rider.

I confess. I bought a life insurance policy with a chronic illness rider. I figured I'd buy one for myself because I'd heard so many good things about them from all the different insurance companies selling them. So, I applied for one and was approved with the preferred rates.

But then I read it.
And I was shocked.

I bought a policy with a $250,000 death benefit. I thought that meant that when I needed long-term care, I would receive $250,000 in long-term care benefits, payable at $5,000 per month for 50 months.

I was wrong.
The long-term care benefits were UNKNOWN.
The long-term care benefits would be determined at the time of claim.

The insurance company considered the "chronic illness benefit" a prepayment of the death benefit. When the "chronic illness" claim is made, the death benefit is re-calculated to its "present value" before calculating the monthly benefit amount.

For example, if the death benefit is $250,000 and I file a "chronic illness" claim, and if I have, for instance, at that time, an 8-year life expectancy, the death benefit would be decreased from $250,000 to about $170,000.

($170,000 today equals about $250,000 eight years from now, assuming current interest rates of 5% per year.)

Since the death benefit would be decreased to only $170,000, my monthly "long-term care" benefit would be only $3,400. I would also permanently forfeit the $80,000 "shrinkage".

But it gets even worse. The policy would also reduce the $170,000 death benefit by the present value of the future premiums, resulting in an even smaller death benefit and smaller monthly benefit.

For example, if the present value of the 8 years of future premiums were $30,000, the $170,000 death benefit would be reduced to $140,000, and the monthly benefit would be only $2,800.

I applied for a $250,000 lifetime benefit with a $5,000 monthly benefit. After reading the policy, I learned I might only get a $140,000 lifetime benefit with a $2,800 monthly benefit.

It might have been an OK life insurance policy, but it was a horrible way to plan for long-term care. That's why I canceled my life insurance policy with a chronic illness rider. **Sadly, most of the hybrids sold today are just like this one I cancelled: universal life insurance with a chronic illness rider.**

LTC BENEFITS ARE EQUAL TO THE DEATH BENEFIT

Permanent life insurance is any life insurance intended to remain in-force for as long as you live. Permanent life insurance is A LOT more expensive than long-term care insurance. Why? Because everyone will die. The chance of needing long-term care is lower than the chance of dying.

There are a lot of permanent life insurance policies for sale today where the entire death benefit can be used for long-term care expenses. That might be a good life insurance policy, but that's probably not a good way to plan for long-term care.

I used to participate in a few "insurance agent forums" online. We ask each other questions, debate different things, and share ideas. Several years ago, one of the agents posted that a couple, both age 59, had recently asked him for some long-term care insurance quotes. He gave them a quote for long-term care insurance, and he also gave them a quote for permanent life insurance. He said they could each get a million dollars of life insurance for the same price as a long-term care insurance policy, so they bought life insurance instead of long-term care insurance.

I challenged him. I posted, "That is impossible! There's no way they can get a million dollars' worth of life insurance for the same price as a long-term care insurance policy." I asked him to "show his work" and post the quotes to prove his statement.

He did. As I suspected, he was NOT comparing apples-to-apples. The life insurance policies he quoted them did not have any inflation protection. The long-term care insurance quotes he gave them included a 5% compound inflation protection rider.

The long-term care insurance policies he quoted for them started with $864,000 in benefits. The 5% compound inflation protection rider would double the benefits to over $1.7 million within 15 years. The benefits would double again to over $3.4 million within another 15 years.

If he'd done a fair comparison and quoted the long-term care insurance policies with NO inflation protection, this couple could have purchased $1,000,000 of long-term care insurance benefits for each spouse for about one-third the cost of the life insurance policies.

That's why I stated above, "Permanent life insurance is A LOT more expensive than long-term care insurance."

If $1,000,000 of permanent life insurance will pay no more than $1,000,000 of long-term care benefits, the life insurance policy is giving you NO leverage. You're buying expensive permanent life insurance to pay for your future long-term care expenses.

Permanent life insurance is usually not the most effective or efficient way to plan for long-term care.

If you want $1,000,000 of long-term care benefits, wouldn't it be better if you only needed to buy $100,000 of permanent life insurance and still be able to get $1,000,000 of long-term care benefits? Or more? Keep reading, and I'll show you how!

LTC BENEFITS ARE GREATER THAN THE DEATH BENEFIT (BEST)

For long-term care planning, the best Life/LTC hybrids are the ones that will pay long-term care benefits that are 3x, 4x, 5x, or even up to 10x the death benefit.

Since life insurance is more expensive than long-term care insurance, if you're interested in a Life/LTC hybrid, **you are better off buying one with a death benefit as low as possible and LTCi benefits as high as possible.**

#1 reason most people should NOT buy a Life/LTC hybrid

The #1 reason most (not all, but most) people should NOT buy a Life/LTC hybrid is because these policies do not qualify for long-term care partnership programs.

Most retirees and near-retirees should plan for long-term care by buying a long-term care partnership policy. LTC partnership policies are the most affordable way for the middle class to protect their assets from long-term care expenses, Medicaid spend-down, and Medicaid estate recovery.

If your long-term care partnership policy runs out of benefits, you can protect *some/most/all* of your assets from Medicaid. How much of your assets are protected depends upon how much your policy pays out in benefits. The higher the amount of LTCi benefits you purchase, the higher the amount of assets protected from Medicaid.

If you own a hybrid and it runs out of long-term care benefits, you will not have any assets protected from Medicaid.

5 reasons someone SHOULD buy a Life/LTC hybrid

Even though most retirees and near-retirees would be better off owning a long-term care partnership policy, there are a few reasons why a Life/LTC hybrid might be a better fit for some people.

1) <u>Health:</u> Life/LTC hybrids tend to have more lenient underwriting than traditional long-term care insurance policies. If you cannot qualify for traditional long-term care insurance, you may be able to qualify for a Life/LTC hybrid or an Annuity/LTC hybrid.

2) <u>If premiums are comparable:</u> Hybrids tend to be priced 2x to 4x higher than traditional long-term care insurance. However, there are some situations where a hybrid might cost only slightly more than a traditional long-term care insurance policy. If the hybrid premium is only a bit more, it may make sense to go with the hybrid because of the potential death benefit and the level premiums. If you are seriously considering a hybrid, make sure you read the chapter entitled "Hybrids! Hybrids! Hybrids!" You should especially read the section "What makes a hybrid good or not-so-good?"

3) <u>International benefits:</u> Most traditional long-term care insurance policies only pay benefits for care received in the United States. A few traditional LTCi policies will pay benefits for care received in the U.S., Canada, and the U.K. If it's essential for you to receive care in other countries, you may be better off buying a Life/LTC hybrid that has good international benefits.

4) <u>Paying family members to provide care:</u> Most traditional LTCi policies do NOT allow family members to be paid to provide care for you. If it's very important to have a family member provide care, you may be more interested in a

Life/LTC hybrid. Some hybrids will allow for 100% of the monthly benefit to be payable "in cash" that can be used in any way you want, including paying family members to care for you.

5) <u>Limited Premium Payments:</u> Would you like to pay for your long-term care coverage in one lump sum? Or would you prefer to pay your premium for only 10 years while in your peak earning years and then have a policy that is paid up for life? Most traditional long-term care insurance policies have premiums that are renewed every year. The premiums are payable for life or until you receive benefits (in most cases). If you'd prefer a policy that is "paid up" with premiums for only a fixed number of years, then a Life/LTC hybrid may be the better choice.

Annuity with some kind of a rider

Annuities are confusing. Annuities are especially confusing when purchased in the context of planning for long-term care. Five main types of annuities are often sold as a way to "plan for long-term care." In the following few pages, I'll explain each, starting with the "worst for planning for long-term care" and leading to the "best for planning for long-term care."

AN ANNUITY WITH A WAIVER OF SURRENDER CHARGE FOR NURSING HOME CARE (WORST)

Several years ago, a man emailed asking me for some quotes on long-term care insurance. I called him about 30 minutes later, and he said, "I don't need the quotes anymore. I've already got long-term care insurance." I thought, "That was fast!" I said that I might be able to get something better for him. "What kind of long-term care insurance do you have?"

He said, "I have two $50,000 annuities. If I need to go to a nursing home, the insurance company will waive the surrender charges, and I can withdraw the money from the annuities to pay for the nursing home."

I replied, "That's not really insurance. Insurance is when an insurance company uses its money to pay for your care. All you're doing with the annuity is using your own money to pay for your care. You're self-insuring." He said, "Well, my insurance agent says this is all I need." I'd heard that before. I continued, "Two $50,000 annuities will not pay for care for very long." He replied, "Well, then, I'll just buy another annuity."

I chuckled and politely hung up the phone. Clearly, he didn't get it.

All he had done was take money from a savings account and put it into an annuity. The annuity would grow each year based on whatever interest rate the insurance company was paying at that time. And he would use that money to pay for his care. Clearly, that's not a smart way to plan for long-term care. He probably would have been better off taking the interest earned each year on those annuities to pay the premium for a robust traditional long-term care insurance policy (or better yet, a long-term care partnership policy.)

IMMEDIATE ANNUITY

An immediate annuity is when someone pays a lump sum to an insurance company in exchange for a guaranteed monthly income for life. The older someone is when they buy an immediate annuity, the higher the monthly income.

According to ImmediateAnnuities.com, a 65-year-old male can pay an insurance company $100,000 in exchange for a guaranteed lifetime income of $621 per month.

LONG-TERM CARE INSURANCE NOW!

An 80-year-old male can pay an insurance company $100,000 in exchange for a guaranteed lifetime income of $1,017 per month.

The other day, I was reading a "personal finance" forum I visit now and then. One of the topics was: "Should I buy LTC insurance or an immediate annuity?" The poster wrote:

"I am nearing retirement, and I'm at the optimum age for purchasing LTC insurance… wouldn't it make sense to wait until I get closer to the optimum age of purchasing an immediate annuity (late 70's or 80's)? The immediate annuity income would supplement my pension and social security and put me in a decent facility."

Immediate annuities can make a lot of sense for someone very concerned about "living too long" and outliving other sources of income. The monthly income from an immediate annuity is guaranteed for life. That's the appeal.

However, an immediate annuity is not a good solution for long-term care planning. Immediate annuities don't provide any leverage. With an immediate annuity, all you get is your money back with some interest. For long-term care planning, it's better to keep the money invested in your portfolio and use some of the interest earned to pay for a robust long-term care insurance policy.

Insurance is all about leverage: pay a small premium in exchange for a large payout if the loss occurs.

An immediate annuity is the opposite of leverage: pay a large premium in exchange for a small monthly payout (albeit for life).

There are excellent uses of immediate annuities for retirement planning, but long-term care planning is not one of those.

Doubling Income When Long-Term Care is Needed

Some immediate annuities have special riders that double the monthly income if you start to need long-term care. This annuity is better than nothing for long-term care planning. However, you're still only getting your money back with some interest, just a little faster than a regular immediate annuity.

For long-term care planning, it's better to keep the money invested in your portfolio and use some of the interest earned to pay for a robust long-term care insurance policy rather than just buying a small-ish monthly income.

Deferred Income Annuity (or **QLAC**)

A "deferred income annuity" is when someone pays a lump sum to an insurance company in exchange for a guaranteed monthly income for life. However, the monthly income is _deferred_ until the annuitant reaches a _certain age_.

For example, according to ImmediateAnnuities.com, a 65-year-old male can pay an insurance company $100,000 in exchange for a guaranteed lifetime income, **starting at age 80,** of $2,037 per month.

Deferred income annuities might be an excellent way of supplementing income later in life. However, deferred income annuities are a horrible way to plan for long-term care:

1) The deferred income annuity will pay nothing if care is needed before age 80. Traditional long-term care insurance provides the entire policy benefits from the day you are approved and pay the first premium. There's no vesting period.
2) There is no inflation protection in the monthly income. With traditional long-term care insurance, you can buy inflation protection, and the policy benefits will grow each year to try and keep pace with the increasing cost of care.

3) Two thousand dollars a month doesn't cover much care in today's dollars, let alone fifteen years from now.

For the purposes of long-term care planning, instead of buying a deferred income annuity, wouldn't it make more sense to keep the $100,000 in your investments and use the interest you earn on that to buy robust long-term care insurance? Of course, it would.

What is a QLAC?

QLAC stands for "Qualified Longevity Annuity Contract." It's exactly like a deferred income annuity, except QLACs are funded with money from retirement accounts (e.g., 401k).

QLACs might be an excellent way to supplement income later in life and minimize taxes on retirement accounts. However, just like regular deferred income annuities, QLACs are not a good way to plan for long-term care.

Multiplying the Premium Deposit for Potential LTC Benefits (BEST)

The best kind of annuities for long-term care planning are those that "multiply" your single premium for long-term care. Depending upon how the annuity is set up, you could get potential LTC benefits that are 2x, 3x, or even 4x, depending on what you deposit into the annuity. If you add an inflation protection rider, the potential LTC benefits could grow to 8x or 9x of what you deposit into the annuity.

This sounds too good to be true, right? Why would an insurance company sell a product like this? Here's why:

1) It's low risk to the insurance company. The insurance company uses the money you deposit into the annuity to pay for your care first. The insurance company doesn't use its money to pay you long-term care benefits until the total

value of the annuity has been spent on your care. Depending upon the company and the product, approximately the first 24 months of care are paid from the annuity (your money).
2) They make money on your money. Even though some of these annuities have decent interest rates that grow your annuity value every year, the insurance company still makes a significant profit investing your money.

Why do people buy these annuities?

1) Easy underwriting: These policies are essentially high-deductible policies. The insurance company incurs no risk until at least the 25th month of care. The underwriting is simple and easy. Many people who can't qualify for traditional long-term care insurance can qualify for this type of annuity.
2) Catastrophic coverage: Some of these annuities have very long benefit periods, some as long as 8 years of benefits. Some have no limit on how long LTC benefits can be paid. These annuities are essentially "high deductible catastrophic long-term care insurance policies."
3) Death Benefit: If care is not needed, there is some form of death benefit. With some of these annuities, the death benefit is the single premium plus interest. The death benefit is sometimes lower due to monthly "LTC rider charges" and policy fees. Make sure you review a full illustration showing the **guaranteed** values over the life of the policy.

What are the advantages and disadvantages of each type of policy?

Advantages of traditional long-term care insurance:

1) When designed properly, traditional long-term care insurance usually provides the most benefit for the least premium compared to all other types of policies.

2) Traditional long-term care insurance policies are easy to tailor to each client's unique situation. There are a lot of options to choose from. Having more choices is good.
3) Traditional long-term care insurance is highly regulated, particularly the Rate Stability Regulation, which is in effect in 41 states.

<u>Disadvantages of traditional long-term care insurance:</u>

1) The biggest disadvantage to traditional long-term care insurance is that it can be very hard to qualify for it. The health underwriting is stringent and often takes several weeks.

Long-term care partnership policies have ALL the same advantages and disadvantages as traditional long-term care insurance. However, long-term care partnership policies have one additional advantage: protecting your assets from Medicaid even if the policy runs out of benefits.

<u>Advantages of recovery policies:</u>

1) The biggest advantage of recovery policies is the underwriting. Most recovery policies use simplified underwriting. Getting approved is easy, and the underwriting process usually takes 5 days or less.
2) Most recovery policies also pay benefits in cash each month. That makes it easier to find care providers.
3) Recovery policies can pay for short-term care situations. For example, if your care were expected to last less than 90 days, a traditional long-term care insurance policy would not pay any benefits. However, a recovery policy could pay benefits in that situation. Most recovery policies allow you to choose a zero-day elimination period.
4) Most recovery policies have a "restoration of benefits" feature. That means you can use the policy, and if you get

all better, the Policy Limit will be restored to its original amount. What's good about this is that it encourages policyholders NOT to delay making a claim. Sometimes, people want to "save up my policy benefits until I really need it." When you've got a policy with a zero-day elimination period and a restoration of benefits feature, there's no need to try to save up your benefits until you really need it.

Disadvantages of recovery policies:

1) The policy limits on recovery policies are lower than traditional long-term care insurance policies. The highest I've found is a policy that starts with $252,000 of total benefits, which can double over 25 years if inflation protection riders are included.
2) Recovery policies have fewer choices for customizing the policy for each client.
3) Recovery policies don't have as many regulations as traditional long-term care insurance. For example, the Rate Stability Regulation does NOT apply to recovery policies.

Advantages of Life/LTC hybrid policies:

1) If you buy the right kind, the long-term care benefits will be much greater than the death benefit.
2) If you buy the right kind, you can add inflation protection, which can significantly increase the long-term care benefits over your lifetime.
3) If you buy the right kind, the premiums are guaranteed never to go up.
4) If you buy the right kind, the policy will be guaranteed to remain in-force for as long as you live.
5) If you buy the right kind, your heirs will receive the death benefit if you never need care. And the death benefit should be about what you paid in premium.

Disadvantages to Life/LTC hybrid policies:

1) If you buy the right kind of Life/LTC hybrid, there's only one disadvantage to these policies: the cost. In some cases, the premiums are much higher than a comparable traditional long-term care insurance policy (with no death benefit.)

Before buying a Life/LTC hybrid policy, read the section in this book entitled "How to compare Life/LTC hybrids with traditional LTCi."

Advantages of Annuity/LTC hybrid policies:

1) If you buy the right kind of Annuity/LTC hybrid, the potential long-term care benefits should be significantly greater than the single premium deposit you put into the annuity.
2) If you buy the right kind of Annuity/LTC hybrid, the underwriting should be very easy. It's usually just a health interview done over the phone or via Zoom with a nurse from the insurance company. Getting approved is easy, and the underwriting process usually takes 5 days or less.
3) The better Annuity/LTC hybrids have a death benefit if you never need care.
4) The better Annuity/LTC hybrids have cash value so that if you decide to surrender the policy, you can get some/most/all your single premium back, minus surrender charges.

Disadvantages to Annuity/LTC hybrid policies:

1) The only disadvantage is the single, lump-sum, premium deposit. The more you put into the annuity, the greater the LTC benefits. The less you put into the annuity, the lower the LTC benefits will be.

Sometimes 2 policies are better than 1

It can sometimes make sense to buy two different types of policies. You can get better benefits for equal or less premium than just one policy. Here are three examples:<u>Example 1:</u> Some traditional LTCi policies have large discounts when a long elimination period (deductible) is chosen. Lengthening the elimination period to 180 days can reduce the premium by as much as 20% or more. Those savings could purchase a meaningful recovery policy covering most (maybe all) of the first 180 days of care.

<u>Example 2:</u> With some Annuity/LTC hybrids, the long-term care benefits payable for the first 24 months of care are lower than the long-term care benefits payable after that. A recovery policy could be purchased to help fill that gap during those first 24 months of care. Also, using this strategy, the amount of funds put into the Annuity/LTC hybrid could be lowered.

Example 3: If, due to health reasons, you are only able to qualify for a recovery policy, it might make sense to buy two recovery policies. You can buy one policy from one company and a second policy from another company.

Chapter 6
Hybrids! Hybrids! Hybrids!

"A-to-Z"

FINANCIAL REPRESENTATIVE	RETIREMENT SPECIALIST
CERTIFIED PLANNER	WEALTH MANAGER
FINANCIAL PROFESSIONAL	SENIOR PLANNING SPECIALIST
CERTIFIED ADVISOR	INSURANCE PLANNING SPECIALIST
INVESTMENT ADVISOR	RETIREMENT ADVISOR
WEALTH PLANNER	INSURANCE PROFESSIONAL
FINANCIAL PLANNING SPECIALIST	SENIOR ADVISOR
CERTIFIED CARE PLANNER	RETIREMENT PLANNER
INVESTMENT PROFESSIONAL	FINANCIAL SPECIALIST
CERTIFIED WEALTH PROFESSIONAL	FINANCIAL PLANNER
FINANCIAL ADVISOR	ASSET PROTECTION SPECIALIST
CERTIFIED RETIREMENT COUNSELOR	RETIREMENT ADVISOR...

So many different titles!!! It is so confusing!

And the confusing titles are followed by even more confusing letters. There is a veritable alphabet soup of letters after everyone's name!

Let's simplify it. Let's call this person in your life your:

"A-to-Z"

If you ask your "A-to-Z" about long-term care insurance, they will probably quote you a cash-value life insurance policy with some type of rider. Remember, the policy your "A-to-Z" shows you may not be the best long-term care planning solution for you. It may be the only product (or one of only a few long-term care products) your "A-to-Z" can offer.

Here is a true story.

A few years ago, I was contacted by a 57-year-old man wanting to buy long-term care insurance. He said he had recently married, and his wife already owned a long-term care insurance policy. She purchased her LTCi policy years ago and wanted him to get a policy.

He asked his "A-to-Z" for a quote for long-term care insurance, and his "A-to-Z" said it would cost $7,500 per year for 10 years for $250,000 in long-term care benefits. He thought that it was expensive, so he contacted me and asked me to find something better for him. I asked him to send me the quote his "A-to-Z" had given him so that I could try to compare "apples to apples."

I have heard 100's of stories like this.
People walk into their "A-to-Z's" office asking for long-term care insurance and come out with information about cash-value life insurance.

Remember that this man asked his "A-to-Z" for a quote for long-term care insurance. The "A-to-Z" quoted him a cash-value life insurance policy.

In this case, the quote the "A-to-Z" gave him was a life insurance policy with a $250,000 death benefit. The policy had a "Living Benefits" rider. This "Living Benefits" rider would allow a portion of the death benefit to be paid after a "qualifying event."

What was the "qualifying event"? If he was confined to a nursing home for at least six consecutive months and was expected to be permanently confined to the nursing home.

Remember, he asked his "A-to-Z" for a quote for long-term care insurance.

Most long-term care insurance policies pay benefits for care received at home. This "living benefits" rider paid nothing for care at home.

Most long-term care insurance policies allow the policyholder to receive benefits while transitioning from home care to facility care and back to home care. That is what happened with my mother-in-law. She started receiving her care at home, transitioned to an assisted-living facility, and then moved into my home when COVID hit. This "living benefits" rider his "A-to-Z" quoted for him would only pay benefits if he were PERMANENTLY CONFINED to a nursing home.

Most long-term care insurance policies have a 90-day elimination period (aka deductible). The elimination period can be satisfied with care received at home, in a facility, or any combination of the two. This "living benefits" rider required 180 days of continuous confinement in a nursing home before it would pay any benefits.

Most long-term care insurance policies pay benefits for care, even if you are expected to recover. This "living benefits" rider would only pay benefits if he were expected to be permanently confined in the nursing home for the rest of his life.

Most long-term care insurance policies have inflation protection. This policy had no inflation protection.

He asked for long-term care insurance.
He was quoted an expensive, cash-value life insurance policy with a mediocre nursing home benefit.

After I pointed out the flaws of this policy to him, he told his "A-to-Z" that he did not want it. The "A-to-Z" said that she had made a mistake. She had intended to quote him a different policy with a better "living benefits" rider.

This second policy was about $1,000 more per year in premium. I reviewed this second policy for him and explained that, in some ways, it was worse than the first one.

1) This second policy was guaranteed to stay in-force only until age 92. If he lived to age 93, the policy could lapse. Even if he paid all the premiums on time every year, the policy could lapse after age 92. If the policy lapsed, he would receive NOTHING from the policy.

No death benefit.
No long-term care benefits.
No cash value.
Nothing. Nada. Zilch. Zero. NOTHING.

2) His beneficiary would only receive the full $250,000 if he died while the policy was in-force AND without him needing any long-term care. If he needed long-term care, the death benefit would be adjusted at that time. The illustration stated: "For the purpose of benefit payments, the Lifetime Benefit is determined at the time of claim." That means the Lifetime Benefit (aka death benefit) would be adjusted when a long-term care claim is submitted. If his life expectancy is long, they could reduce the death benefit significantly, even by half. Reducing the death benefit would also reduce the monthly benefit. If they cut the death benefit in half ($125,000), the monthly benefit would be only $2,500. Can you imagine buying a policy with $250,000 in benefits and then being told that the policy will pay only half that amount at the time of claim? That is how this policy works.

3) There was no inflation protection.

4) He could get much better long-term care benefits for about $200 per month with a traditional LTCi policy with inflation protection.

5) Instead of paying $85,000 for the life insurance policy, he could keep the $85,000 invested. Earning 3% on the $85,000 would be enough to pay the long-term care insurance premium every year.

6) Lastly, he could deduct the long-term care insurance premium from his federal income taxes because he was self-employed. The premium for the life insurance policy would not be tax-deductible.

Clearly, he would be much better off with a traditional long-term care insurance policy than buying an expensive, cash-value life insurance policy with mediocre long-term care benefits.

That is why I stated at the beginning of this section:

"Keep in mind, the policy your "A-to-Z" shows you may not be the best long-term care solution for you. It may be the only product (or one of only a few long-term care products) your "A-to-Z" can offer."

"Local long-term care insurance specialist"

I have a client who bought an excellent long-term care partnership policy in 2018 when she was in her mid-fifties. Her policy had a starting monthly benefit of $3,720 and a starting policy limit of $219,000. Her policy also has a 5% compound inflation benefit with no cap. That means that for as long as she lives, her monthly benefit and policy limit will grow by 5% compounded growth every year. The growth in the benefits each year does NOT make the premium go up each year. The annual 5% compounded growth is included in her premium from the start. Her premium was about $3,000 per year.

Since her policy is a Long-Term Care Partnership policy, it has "dollar-for-dollar" asset protection. That means that if her policy were to run out of benefits, she could apply for Medicaid to pay for her care, and Medicaid would allow her to keep, in countable assets, an amount equal to whatever her policy had paid in benefits. For example, if she needs care and receives $800,000 in benefits from the policy, which then runs out of benefits, she could apply for Medicaid and keep $800,000 in savings!

Last year, she moved from Indiana to South Carolina. She decided to meet with an "A-to-Z" who could help guide her as she nears retirement. She mentioned to the "A-to-Z" that she had purchased an excellent long-term care insurance policy and was all set in that area. The "A-to-Z" recommended she speak with a "local long-term care insurance specialist" to ensure her policy was everything she thought it was. She agreed to meet with the "local long-term care insurance specialist."

After reviewing her current policy, the "local long-term care insurance specialist" told her that she should apply for a different policy and cancel the policy she had purchased from me. This new policy was a life insurance policy with a long-term care rider. It had a one-time, single premium of $100,000 and no ongoing premiums.

Why did the "long-term care insurance specialist" recommend she drop her long-term care partnership policy?

At the time of their meeting, my client's long-term care partnership policy had a monthly benefit of $4,522.

The life insurance policy with the long-term care rider would have a long-term care monthly benefit of only $3,600.

Her long-term care partnership policy had a 5% compound inflation protection rider with no cap. Her benefits would grow by 5%

compound every year for as long as she had the policy. Her benefits would even grow while she was on claim receiving care.

The life insurance policy had a 3% compound inflation protection rider, and the inflation protection lasted only 20 years. That means that the long-term care benefits would only grow for 20 years. There would be no growth in the long-term care monthly benefit after 20 years.

If she went on claim twenty years from now, her long-term care partnership policy would pay long-term care benefits totaling $739,980 over five years.

If she went on claim twenty years from now, the life insurance policy would pay long-term care benefits totaling only $317,750 over five years.

Her long-term care partnership policy would have more than TWICE the long-term care benefits!

Why would the "local long-term care insurance specialist" recommend that she pay $100,000 for a policy with less than half the benefits?

Keep reading. It gets worse:

- The "local long-term care insurance specialist" told my client that a policy purchased outside of South Carolina might not be valid in South Carolina.
- The "specialist" told my client that South Carolina does not have a long-term care partnership program and that she might have to move back to Indiana to get the full benefits from the policy.
- The "specialist" told my client that long-term care partnership policies are no longer being sold across the country.

My client was genuinely concerned by these statements. Fortunately, all three statements the "specialist" made were 100% FALSE. I shared the truth with my client, specifically:

- All long-term care insurance policies pay benefits in all 50 states, no matter where the policy was purchased.
- All states with long-term care partnership programs honor every other state's long-term care partnership program, except California. California is the only state that does not honor other states' long-term care partnership programs.
- Most long-term care insurance policies sold today ARE long-term care partnership policies.

To help ease my client's concerns, I sent her direct links to the specific pages on the Indiana and South Carolina government websites, refuting what the "specialist" had told her.

The "local long-term care insurance specialist" was either lying or ignorant. Since I chose to believe the best about people, I assumed this specialist was just ignorant. Thankfully, my client reached out to me before making a big mistake.

IF YOU ASK 20 INSURANCE AGENTS FOR INFORMATION ON LONG-TERM CARE INSURANCE, 19 WILL GIVE YOU INFORMATION ON LIFE INSURANCE.

When you say "long-term care insurance" to an insurance agent or an "A-to-Z," they usually hear "life insurance." Sadly, much of what is published on the internet makes it even harder for consumers to receive a fair comparison between long-term care insurance and cash-value life insurance. A common theme I have seen on the internet is for insurance agents to exaggerate the cost of traditional long-term care insurance premiums to make cash-value life insurance seem more affordable.

For example, I recently read an article on the website of one of the most reputable retirement planning publications. The writer of the article was an "A-to-Z." The article compared traditional long-term care insurance versus life insurance with a long-term care rider. He wrote that a typical long-term care insurance policy for a couple costs $12,000 per year for only 3 years of benefits for each spouse. I was surprised by that statement. I have thousands of clients across the country. Most of my clients buy a lot more than 3 years of benefits, and most of my clients pay a lot less than $12,000 per year.

I was curious about which long-term care insurance policy was so expensive. I searched for the writer of the article on the insurance commissioner's website to see which long-term care insurance companies he sold policies for. Surprisingly, I discovered he was not even licensed to sell long-term care insurance. He was licensed to sell life insurance. He was appointed with 17 different insurance companies. All those companies sell life insurance with some kind of rider. None of those companies sell long-term care insurance. He was not licensed to sell long-term care insurance with any company. Why would he say that long-term care insurance costs $12,000 per year when he is not even appointed with one long-term care insurance company?

Not surprisingly, in the article, the "A-to-Z" wrote that cash value life insurance usually costs about the same as, or just a little bit more than, traditional long-term care insurance.

Do not trust anything you read on the internet about how much traditional long-term care insurance costs.

Get real quotes at LTCShop.com and click on Policy Finder. Answer a few basic questions and one of my associates or I will email you a customized quote within one business day.

No phone is required.
No need to give your name.
No need to speak with anyone.

Use-it-or-lose-it is NOT a flaw; it's a feature

If someone tells you that you should dismiss traditional long-term care insurance because it is "use it or lose it," that person is not using the logical side of their brain.

Auto insurance is "use it or lose it."
Homeowner's insurance is "use it or lose it."
Medical insurance is "use it or lose it."
Disability insurance is "use it or lose it."
Nearly every form of insurance is "use it or lose it."

Would anyone say, "Don't buy auto insurance because if you don't get in a car crash, you won't get anything out of the policy."

Would anyone say, "Don't buy medical insurance because if you don't have major surgery, you won't get much out of the policy."

That makes NO sense. Yet that is what "A-to-Zs" tell people every day. You can read it all over the internet.

<u>Use it or lose it is a feature, not a flaw.</u>

"Use it or lose it" is a good thing. It means you are not paying extra for a death benefit, which would be wiped out if you do need care.

You see, hybrids are "if you use it, you'll lose it" policies. Read that again:

Hybrids are "if you use it, you'll lose it" policies.

If you use the hybrid for long-term care, you'll lose all (or nearly all) of the death benefit anyway. So why pay 2x to 4x MORE premium for a hybrid? Why waste money paying extra for a death benefit you might not get?

If you are healthy enough to qualify for a traditional long-term care insurance policy, nine times out of ten you will be better off buying a traditional long-term care insurance policy rather than a hybrid.

Some hybrids can turn into NOTHING! NOTHING! NOTHING!

(even if you pay your premium on time every year!)

Many hybrids can lapse even if you pay the premiums on time every year. Hybrids are sold as the best of all worlds with three different ways to benefit from the policy:

- ➢ If you need cash, you can cancel the policy and get your cash.
- ➢ If you need long-term care, you can use the death benefit to pay for your long-term care.
- ➢ If you do not need long-term care, then your heirs will get the tax-free death benefit.
- ❖ OR, you and your heirs could get NOTHING from the policy.

Unfortunately, this is a very real possibility, and it is rarely discussed.

Even if you pay your premiums on time every year and NEVER miss a payment, the policy could lapse.

This is not true for every hybrid. But this is true for most of the hybrids that have been sold over the past few years. Again, it is not every hybrid, but many hybrid policies <u>can lapse</u>.

If the policy lapses, you will lose every penny you put into the policy. If the policy lapses, you will get NOTHING from the policy:

- No cash value.

- No long-term care benefits.
- No death benefit.

Most hybrid policies are NOT guaranteed to stay in-force for the rest of your life. They might lapse when you reach age 90, or 85, or 80, or even sooner than that. The only way to know that the policy will remain in-force for life is if you look at the page of the illustration that shows "**guaranteed values**." That page will show you the guaranteed death benefit every year of the policy. If the death benefit is zero before you reach age 100, that means you could lose everything you put into the policy and get NOTHING out of the policy. All your premiums would be wasted. (The better hybrids even guarantee the death benefit through age 120!)

If the "A-to-Z" cannot show you the page of the illustration with the guaranteed premium and the guaranteed death benefit through age 100 (or 120), then that product is not the best product for long-term care purposes.

If you need life insurance, do NOT buy a hybrid.

Every week, I read somewhere on the internet that the perfect candidate to buy a hybrid is someone who needs long-term care insurance and has a need for life insurance. Just the opposite is true.

If you need life insurance, do NOT buy a hybrid.

Why?

If you buy a hybrid and need long-term care, the death benefit will be depleted by paying for the long-term care. If you need life insurance and you need long-term care insurance, you should buy two separate policies.

What makes a "hybrid" good or "not-so-good"

A "hybrid" may be a great solution for you when planning for long-term care. Here are some of the things I look for when determining if a "hybrid" is a good solution for long-term care planning or a "not-so-good" solution. It should have:

- a death benefit that is **guaranteed** through age 120 (or at least through age 100).
- premiums that are **guaranteed** never to go up,
- **guaranteed** inflation protection, and
- leverage.

The more leverage a hybrid offers, the better it is. What do I mean by "leverage?"

How much potential long-term care benefit can you receive for each dollar you pay in premium?

How many times greater are the long-term care benefits compared to the life insurance death benefit?

When a hybrid is the right solution for one of my clients, my goal is to design it in such a way as to minimize their out-of-pocket premiums and maximize the potential long-term care benefits.

Chapter 7
Shopping for Long-Term Care Coverage

Your health history is THE MOST CRITICAL FACTOR

There are a lot of factors that go into determining which policy I recommend for each client:

1) your age when you apply
2) your state of residence
3) if you live alone or have a partner
4) the amount of benefits you want to buy

But the single most critical factor is your health history. Five types of policies can help pay for long-term care. Your health history may prevent you from purchasing some types of policies.

With some health conditions, it is easier to qualify for a traditional long-term care insurance policy compared to a Life/LTC hybrid.

With other health conditions, it is easier to qualify for a Life/LTC hybrid compared to a traditional long-term care insurance policy.

With some health conditions, you may not be able to qualify for a traditional long-term care insurance policy or a Life/LTC hybrid. Still, you may qualify for a Recovery policy or an Annuity with an LTC rider.

After speaking with a new client, the very first thing I do is review the underwriting guides for the various products I sell. If my client has some health issues, I may find that, out of the 15 different policies I offer, they may only qualify for three of them.

> *The healthier you are when you apply for a policy, the more choices you will have.*

When you buy long-term care insurance, you should be saying to yourself, "I feel too young and too healthy to buy this right now."

FAMILY HISTORY AND LONG-TERM CARE INSURANCE

Long-term care insurance companies are usually NOT concerned with your family history. I will hear people say, "Most of my relatives just died of a heart attack before they turned 70. I won't need long-term care." According to the actuaries and underwriters, your family history does not really matter. Today, we survive what used to kill our forebears.

People who choose to work with me to help them apply for long-term care insurance are often surprised that the applications ask little about family history.

Of course, there are a few health conditions that can be passed from one generation to the next. These can be of concern to long-term care insurance companies, particularly Huntington's disease, ataxia, and polycystic kidney disease.

What about a family history of Alzheimer's or dementia? This is something that long-term care insurance companies can be genuinely concerned about. But, late in life, dementia is not unusual. The biggest concern to the underwriters is early onset dementia and Alzheimer's. If you have parents or siblings who have been diagnosed at an early age with dementia or Alzheimer's, you may still be able to qualify for long-term care insurance. That is why I work with a lot of different companies. Every company is a little different in how they look at various health histories.

3 TYPES OF UNDERWRITING: FULL, MODIFIED, AND SIMPLIFIED

There are three underwriting methods insurance companies use to determine if you can qualify for a particular policy.

- Full underwriting
- Modified underwriting and
- Simplified underwriting

Full underwriting means the insurance company will review your medical records from your primary care doctor. If you've seen a specialist in the past few years, they will probably also review those medical records. They will also do a "health interview" either over the phone (or in person). The "health interview" includes a lot of health questions and, depending on your age, a short cognitive quiz. The insurance company may also request a copy of your "Prescription Drug Report," your ICD-10 medical treatment codes, and an MIB (Medical Information Bureau) report. The insurance company collects all this information. You do not have to get it for them. All you do is sign a HIPAA form authorizing the insurance company to gather the information. *Occasionally*, they may request a blood sample, a urinalysis, and a driving record.

Modified underwriting is like Full underwriting; however, the insurance company does not request any medical records.

Simplified underwriting usually includes a copy of your "Prescription Drug Report", your ICD-10 treatment codes, and an MIB report. Simplified underwriting usually has a short "yes or no" application with several health questions.

Each policy uses _one_ of these three types of underwriting.

You might have a health condition that prevents you from purchasing a policy that uses Full underwriting. However, you may be able to qualify for a policy that uses Modified or Simplified underwriting.

The reverse can be true also. You may qualify for a policy that uses Full underwriting but not for a policy that uses Modified or Simplified underwriting.

For example, a policy that uses Modified underwriting may have a health question that makes someone uninsurable if they had a certain type of cancer in the past five years. However, a policy that uses Simplified underwriting might insure that same person if the cancer was successfully treated only three years ago. A policy that uses Full underwriting might even insure that person if the cancer was successfully treated less than three years ago.

My job is to "thread the needle" and pinpoint exactly which policies you can qualify for based on your unique health history.

A better analogy may be to say that I am a "long-term care insurance" matchmaker. I will help you find your "perfect match."

POTENTIAL PITFALLS OF EMPLOYER-SPONSORED INSURANCE

Just because a policy is offered through your employer does NOT mean it is the best policy for you. This is particularly true if your employer is offering a "hybrid" policy because "hybrids" can be two to three times more expensive than a traditional long-term care insurance policy.

A healthy couple can usually get better benefits for less premium by purchasing a long-term care policy on their own rather than buying a policy through an employer.

Individually purchased long-term care policies usually offer:
- Preferred health discounts that can save as much as 25% and
- Marital discounts that can save as much as 40%. (Marital discounts are even given to domestic partners in most states).

The biggest disadvantage to watch out for is that group long-term care insurance policies are usually NOT Long-Term Care Partnership policies.

Most employer-sponsored policies are hybrid and do not usually have any inflation protection. Policies that have no inflation protection become less valuable over time because they do not keep up with the increasing cost of care.

If you are an employer or an H.R. executive, what should you do?

Why not send your employees to LTCShop.com?

We can obtain an employer discount from the top long-term care insurance companies. We will create a microsite for your employees, and we will give your employees the same personalized concierge long-term care insurance design we give all our clients.

How to compare "hybrids" with traditional LTCi

Probably the hardest thing for a consumer to do is to try to compare a traditional long-term care insurance policy with a "hybrid."

Which type of policy is better?
How can you be sure you are choosing the right one?

Recently, I provided some quotes to a man in his mid-fifties. He wanted a policy that would start with about $400,000 of benefits and would grow every year to try to keep pace with the increasing cost of care. He was extremely healthy and qualified for preferred rates.

I found an excellent policy for him that would start with about $370,000 of benefits, paying about $5,000 for each month that he needed care. Those amounts would grow every year by 3% compounding. The growth in the benefits each year would not make the premium go up each year. That inflation growth was built into the premium from the beginning. His premium was going to be $212 per month.

I followed up with him, and he told me that he had applied for a hybrid with a death benefit. I said, "Hybrids are usually two to three times more expensive than a traditional long-term care insurance policy. Why did you buy the hybrid?" He said that the hybrid was about $15 per month ***cheaper*** than the traditional long-term care policy I'd quoted for him, AND the hybrid had a death benefit. I replied, "If that is true, I want to learn more about that policy because I will sell a bunch of them. But we are probably not comparing apples-to-apples. Can you send me the illustration you were given?"

He sent me the illustration. After reviewing it, I explained to him the benefits he had applied for.

- o I had quoted him a policy with a starting monthly benefit of $5,000. That means that for each month that he needed care, the policy would pay up to $5,000. The hybrid he applied for had a starting monthly benefit of only $2,500.
- o I had quoted him a policy that would start with $370,000 of long-term care benefits. The hybrid he had applied for started with only $150,000 of long-term care benefits.
- o I had quoted him a policy that would grow the long-term care benefits every year by 3% compounding. The hybrid he applied for would increase the long-term care benefits by 3% compound, but the growth would stop after 20 years.
- o The policy I quoted him was guaranteed to have a monthly benefit of $13,281 by age 85, and it would continue to grow every year for as long as he lived. The hybrid he had applied for would have a monthly benefit of only $4,515 by age 75 and would never grow any more than that.

o The policy I quoted him was guaranteed to have a lifetime benefit of $903,670 by age 85, and it would continue to grow every year. The hybrid he had applied for would have a lifetime benefit of only $270,917 by age 75 and would never grow any more than that.

He had no idea the hybrid policy's long-term care benefits were so much lower than the traditional long-term care policy I had quoted for him. He was only looking at the premium.

<u>Here is a simple trick to help you compare a hybrid with traditional long-term care insurance:</u>

Focus on the 3 benefits that "hybrids" and traditional long-term care insurance have in common:

1. **Monthly Benefit**
2. **Lifetime Benefit**
3. **Inflation Benefit**

The Monthly Benefit is the most the "hybrid" will pay for any month that you need care.

The Lifetime Benefit is the most the "hybrid" will pay in long-term care benefits over your lifetime.

The Inflation Benefit is how the Monthly Benefit and the Lifetime Benefit will grow over time to try to keep pace with the increasing cost of care.

Example 1:

Married couple
60-year-old male
60-year old female

Hybrid:
Monthly Benefit: $5,000 per spouse
Lifetime Benefit: $300,000 per spouse
Inflation Benefit: 3% compound for life
Combined annual premium: $13,678 to age 95

Traditional Long-Term Care Insurance policy:
Monthly Benefit: $5,100 per spouse
Lifetime Benefit: $310,250 per spouse (plus an additional shared $310,250)
Inflation Benefit: 3% compound for life
Combined annual premium: $5,866 for life

For this couple, the hybrid costs $7,812 more per year than the traditional long-term care insurance policy.

By pinpointing exactly how much more the hybrid costs each year versus the traditional long-term care insurance policy, this couple can determine if the extra $7,812 per year is worth the extra benefits that are included in the hybrid.

If this couple needs more life insurance, it might make more sense to buy a traditional long-term care insurance policy and a separate life insurance policy rather than buying a hybrid.

Example 2:

Single, 50-year old female

Hybrid:
Monthly Benefit: $5,000
Lifetime Benefit: $388,105
Inflation Benefit: 3% compound for life
Annual premium: $6,629 for life

Traditional Long-Term Care Insurance policy:
Monthly Benefit: $4,800
Lifetime Benefit: $350,400
Inflation Benefit: 3% compound for life
Annual premium: $3,308 for life

For this woman, the hybrid costs $3,321 more per year than the traditional long-term care insurance policy.

By pinpointing exactly how much more the hybrid costs each year versus the traditional long-term care insurance policy, she can determine if the extra $3,321 per year is worth the extra benefits included in the hybrid.

If she needs more life insurance, it might make more sense to buy a traditional long-term care insurance policy and a separate life insurance policy rather than buying a hybrid.

Example 3:

Single, 55-year-old male

Hybrid:
Monthly Benefit: $5,000
Lifetime Benefit: $388,105
Inflation Benefit: 3% compound for life
Annual premium: $5,696 for life

Traditional Long-Term Care Insurance policy:
Monthly Benefit: $5,100
Lifetime Benefit: $372,300
Inflation Benefit: 3% compound for life
Annual premium: $2,419 for life

For this man, the hybrid costs $3,277 more per year than the traditional long-term care insurance policy.

By pinpointing exactly how much more the hybrid costs each year versus the traditional long-term care insurance policy, he can determine if the extra $3,277 per year is worth the extra benefits included in the hybrid.

If he needs more life insurance, it might make more sense to buy a traditional long-term care insurance policy and a separate life insurance policy rather than buying a hybrid.

<u>Half-Truth</u>: "If you don't want to pay for expensive long-term care insurance, you should consider buying a hybrid."

<u>The other half of the truth</u>: "Yes, traditional long-term care insurance is expensive, but hybrids are often A LOT more expensive than traditional long-term care insurance."

As you can see from the examples provided, when comparing similar long-term care benefits, hybrids can be two times, sometimes three times, more expensive than a traditional long-term care insurance policy.

When comparing hybrids to traditional long-term care insurance, there are two other VERY IMPORTANT questions you must ask:

1) "Is the Inflation Benefit growth guaranteed every year, OR is it just an estimate?" With most traditional long-term care insurance policies, the Inflation Benefit growth is guaranteed every year for as long as you live. With some hybrids, the growth in the benefits is just a projection and is not guaranteed.

2) "Is the hybrid guaranteed to remain in-force through my 100th birthday?" If the hybrid is not guaranteed to remain in-force through age 100, you should NOT consider buying that hybrid as a plan for long-term care. Many hybrids are not guaranteed to remain in-force for life. If you buy a hybrid to help fund your future long-term care

needs and the policy lapses before you need care, you'll get NOTHING from the policy.

How to **INCORRECTLY** compare "hybrids" with traditional LTCi

Example:

A woman in her mid-fifties read something I had tweeted, and she contacted me asking for advice about a policy she had just applied for. She'd met with "A-to-Z," who showed her two different policies.

Each policy was nearly identical in price. One policy was a traditional long-term care insurance policy. It had a Monthly Benefit of $5,000 and a Lifetime Benefit of $250,000. The other policy was a life insurance policy with a rider. The death benefit could be used to pay for long-term care if needed. It also had a Monthly Benefit of $5,000 and a Lifetime Benefit of $250,000. Since it was a life insurance policy, if she never needed long-term care, it would pay a death benefit of $250,000. Since the premiums were nearly identical, it sounded to her like the life insurance policy was the better way to go.

She contacted me because she didn't feel right about the choice; something was gnawing at her. I asked her, "What will the life insurance policy's Monthly Benefit be 5 years from now, 15 years from now, and 25 years from now?" She wasn't sure at first, but after flipping through the pages of the illustration, she noticed that the Monthly Benefit would always be $5,000. It didn't grow.

I then asked her to look at the quote "A-to-Z" gave her for the traditional long-term care insurance policy. I asked her to check if the long-term care insurance policy included any type of inflation benefit. If a long-term care insurance policy contains an Inflation Benefit, the Monthly Benefit and the Lifetime Benefit will grow automatically every year.

The quote the agent gave her for the long-term care insurance policy included a 3% compound Inflation Benefit. That means the Monthly Benefit and the Lifetime Benefit would automatically increase every year by 3% compounded growth. With that policy, the 3% compounded growth each year would not make the premium go up each year. The premium was designed to remain level, even though the benefits were guaranteed to grow every year.

Using a spreadsheet, I calculated for her how much the Monthly Benefit and the Lifetime Benefit would be in 25 years.

The long-term care policy's Monthly Benefit and Lifetime Benefit would more than double over the next 25 years.

Her main reason for buying long-term care coverage was to be able to afford the best possible care, not leave money to an heir. A long-term care policy that grows by 3% compound every year would be better for her than a life insurance policy that didn't grow. She canceled the life insurance policy and purchased a long-term care insurance policy instead.

The "A-to-Z" she was working with should have explained to her that the long-term care insurance benefits would grow every year, but the life insurance policy would not.

The cheat sheet I shared with you at the beginning of this chapter would look something like this for this woman:

Single, 55-year old female

<u>Hybrid:</u>
Monthly Benefit: $5,000
Lifetime Benefit: $240,000
Inflation Benefit: none
Annual premium: $4,195

Traditional Long-Term Care Insurance policy:
Monthly Benefit: $5,100
Lifetime Benefit: $248,200
Inflation Benefit: 3% compound for life
Annual premium: $4,061

~~~~~~~~~~~~~~~~

A few years ago, a woman contacted me asking if I could help her purchase long-term care insurance. She was in her late forties and had some health problems. A life insurance agent told her that she couldn't qualify for a traditional long-term care insurance policy, so he sold her an Indexed Universal Life insurance policy with a "chronic illness" rider.

I told her that there were some good "chronic illness" riders and some "not-so-good" "chronic illness" riders. I asked her to email me the illustration that came with the policy, and I would review it and give her my professional opinion.

Keep in mind that she wanted long-term care coverage. She wanted to make sure her assets were protected for her spouse and her children if she needed long-term care at some point in the future. She already had life insurance, and she didn't need more. Her concern was needing long-term care.

The first thing I looked at in the illustration was when the policy could lapse. Remember, earlier in this chapter, I stated that you MUST ask this question if you're considering buying a "hybrid":

"Is the hybrid guaranteed to remain in-force through my 100th birthday?" If the hybrid is not guaranteed to remain in-force through age 100, you should NOT consider buying that hybrid for the purpose of long-term care planning.

So, that was the first thing I looked at when she sent me her illustration. I wanted to find out if this policy was guaranteed to remain in-force through her 100th birthday.

It wasn't. In fact, the policy was guaranteed to remain in-force only to age 72. The policy could lapse anytime after age 72. At age 73 or thereafter, the policy could lapse, leaving her with ZERO long-term care benefits, ZERO death benefits, and ZERO cash value. All her premiums would be wasted.

~~~~~~~~~~~~~~~~

51-year-old couple in NY asked their "A-to-Z" about long-term care insurance. He told them that each of them should buy a hybrid policy that had $496,800 of long-term care benefits (with no inflation protection). The premium for the wife was $8,955 for 10 years. Total premium of $89,550. The premium for the husband was $9,582 for 10 years. Total premium of $95,820. They contacted me and asked what I recommended they do. I found them the same long-term care benefits for $1,298 per year per spouse. It would take them 71 years to pay more for the traditional long-term care insurance than they would pay for that hybrid. If you consider that they would be losing about $5,000 per year of interest on the money they would have to put in the hybrid, they come out WAY AHEAD buying the traditional policies.

Is a "cash indemnity" policy better or a "reimbursement" policy?

A "cash indemnity" policy is a policy that pays the full monthly benefit each month you qualify for care, regardless of the actual cost of care.

A "reimbursement" policy is a policy that pays **up to** the full monthly benefit each month you qualify for care.

My mother-in-law's policy was a "reimbursement" policy. For years, I have heard people in my industry say, "Reimbursement policies are so hard at the time of claim." They have said, "You have to keep track of all kinds of receipts. It's so much easier to have a cash indemnity policy."

My mother-in-law needed long-term care for about four years. My wife filed a claim each month to get reimbursed for the cost of the care.

There were no receipts. Once a month, the assisted-living facility would mail a statement to my wife detailing the prior month's charges. My wife would upload it to the long-term care insurance company's secure server. About 5 business days later, the insurance company would deposit the amount in my mother-in-law's checking account.

The only time we needed to submit receipts was when the insurance company paid to renovate our bathroom. My mother-in-law moved in with us during COVID, and she needed a walk-in shower. We sent the insurance company the invoice from the contractor for the cost of the labor and the invoice from Home Depot for the shower and tile. They reimbursed nearly the entire cost of the bathroom renovation. To get that, all we had to do was send them two receipts.

When is a cash indemnity better than a reimbursement?
When you want to pay a family member to provide care.

Most long-term care insurance policies do NOT pay benefits for care provided by a family member. The main concerns are fraud and elder abuse. Without any oversight from a third party, it can open the door to fraud. Or the person responsible for providing the care may not be doing the job properly.

With a reimbursement policy, there is always some kind of oversight from a third party (e.g., a licensed CNA or home health aide, a home care agency manager, etc....) With a "cash indemnity" policy, there's an opportunity for the funds to be misused.

If you want the flexibility to pay a family member (or an unlicensed caregiver), then you should buy a policy that pays a "cash indemnity."

Is a monthly benefit better than a daily benefit?

Every long-term care insurance policy has EITHER a daily benefit or a monthly benefit. The daily benefit is the most the policy can pay for each **day** you need care. The monthly benefit is the most the policy can pay for each **month** you need care. For example, a policy with a $200 "daily benefit" is comparable to a policy with a $6,000 "monthly benefit" ($200 x 30 = $6,000).

Which is better? A "daily benefit" or a "monthly benefit"? If you ask 100 insurance professionals which is better, 99 would say "monthly benefit." But, as with most things in life, the more accurate answer is: "It depends."

For care in a facility, a "daily benefit" is better than a "monthly benefit." I will repeat that because you will not find this anywhere on the internet:

For care in a facility, a "daily benefit" is better than a "monthly benefit."

Why? Because a policy with a "daily benefit" will pay more in months that have 31 days. For example, if a policy has a daily benefit of $200, it will pay up to $6,200 in a month with 31 days. A comparable policy with a "monthly benefit" of $6,000 would pay only up to $6,000 even in months with 31 days.

My mother-in-law had a policy with a "daily benefit." When she was in the assisted-living facility, each monthly statement listed the daily charges for room, board, and care services. The daily rate did not change throughout the month. For months that had 31 days, her policy paid more than if she had had a policy with a "monthly benefit".

For home care, a monthly benefit can be better. Here is one ***bad*** example:

Mr. Jones needs a home health aide every day to help him bathe and dress. The home health aide charges him $100 per day. On Tuesdays and Thursdays, Mr. Jones has physical therapy. The therapy costs $250 per visit. His total care expenses are $350 every Tuesday and $350 every Thursday ($100 for the home health aide plus $250 for the physical therapist).

If Mr. Jones' long-term care insurance policy has a daily benefit of $200, he will have to pay $150 out of his own pocket every Tuesday and every Thursday.

If Mr. Jones' long-term care insurance policy has a monthly benefit of $6,000, he will not have to pay anything out of pocket. The total cost of his care, including the physical therapist visits, would be less than $6,000 each month.

The reason I say this is a ***bad*** example is because physical therapy is covered by Medicare (and most medical insurance policies). Why use your long-term care insurance policy to pay for care that Medicare already covers? It is a terrible example, yet this example is often used to explain why a "monthly benefit" is better than a "daily benefit."

Here is a real-life example:
When my sister-in-law passed away, my wife and I flew to New Jersey to spend 5 days with my brother, just to be there for him in any way that we could. My mother-in-law was living with us at the time. We

had a home health aide for several hours every day taking care of her while we worked. For us to fly to New Jersey for the funeral, we needed the home health aide to be with my mother-in-law 24 hours a day. Of course, we had to pay her a lot more than we normally paid her. However, my mother-in-law's policy had a daily benefit. So, for the 5 days we were gone, her policy did not cover the full cost of the care. If she had had a monthly benefit, we would have had less out-of-pocket for those 5 days.

HOW MUCH MORE SHOULD YOU PAY FOR A "MONTHLY BENEFIT"?

Recently, I was comparing policies for a couple, and they were looking at a policy that had a $5,000 monthly benefit. I was recommending they buy a policy with a $170 daily benefit. They told me that they had read on the internet that policies with a monthly benefit are better than policies with a daily benefit. I said, "Well, that depends. That particular policy with the monthly benefit costs 30% MORE premium. If you want to spend 30% more, you can buy a $220 daily benefit for the same price as the other policy with a $5,000 monthly benefit. A $220 daily benefit would, in most months, pay out $6,600." The choice was obvious.

Do not get hung up on "daily vs. monthly." One may be better than the other, but it will depend upon how much extra the policy is with the "monthly benefit" costs.

Is a calendar day elimination period better than a service day?

The "elimination period" is the number of days you receive care before the policy will start to pay benefits. It is like a deductible.

There are two main types of elimination periods: Service day and Calendar day.

A "Service Day" elimination period means that one day of the elimination period is satisfied for each day you receive paid services from a qualified care provider.

A "Calendar Day" elimination period means that one day of the elimination period is satisfied for each day on the calendar that passes, whether you paid someone to care for you or not.

Which is better?

For the care you receive in a facility, there is no difference between "Service Day" and "Calendar Day." Every day you are in the facility would count as one day towards a "calendar day" elimination period or one day towards a "service day" elimination period.

The only time a "calendar day" elimination period is better is if you have someone who will provide free care for you during the elimination period. Free care (provided by a friend or relative) would not count towards a "service day" elimination period.

For home care, a calendar day elimination period can be better. Here is one **bad** example:

If you need help two days per week, it will take 45 weeks to satisfy a "90 service day elimination period."

This is a bad example for a lot of reasons.

First, why would someone need care only two days per week? Long-term care insurance policies pay benefits when the policyholder needs assistance with the Activities of *DAILY* Living. Do we bathe only two days per week? Do we get dressed only two days per week? Do we eat only two days per week? Do we use the toilet only two days per week?

My mother-in-law had a 90-day "service day" elimination period when she needed to use her long-term care policy. We had a home health aide come to the house for a short visit every morning for a few hours. The aide helped her out of bed, helped her shower and dress, made her breakfast, and did some light housekeeping. Even a short visit like that counts as one day towards the elimination period. It did not make sense to have an aide only a few days per week. So, I don't understand why people in my industry say, "What if you need care only two days per week?" That does not make sense.

By hiring a home health aide for a short visit every day, you can satisfy the "service day" elimination period as quickly as possible and with only a little out-of-pocket expense.

Understanding Comdex rankings

Many different agencies rate insurance companies for their financial strength. They all use different criteria and different ranking systems. It is very confusing.

In my opinion, the two most important rating agencies are A.M. Best and S & P. Ideally, you want to buy your long-term care coverage from a company that is ranked at least "A minus" by A.M. Best and S & P.

In my opinion, you should not put a lot of weight on the "Comdex" composite. The Comdex is easily misunderstood by both consumers and "A-to-Zs." The Comdex is not a rating. It is a percentile using the ratings from the rating agencies.

Here is how the Comdex can be easily misunderstood:

Suppose I am a first-year student in college, and I take "Psychology 101". I take the mid-term exam and get 90% of the questions correct. 90% is excellent, right? I got 9 out of every 10 questions correct. My professor gives me an "A-minus." However, half of my classmates scored higher than a 90. The other half scored lower than a 90.

If Comdex were my professor, Comdex would give me a "50", not a "90". Comdex would give me a 50 because 50% of my classmates scored lower than I did, and 50% of my classmates scored higher than I did.

That is why I think the Comdex composite is often misunderstood. A company can have a strong financial rating (e.g., an "A minus") and still get a low Comdex ranking. Unfortunately, when consumers look at the Comdex rankings, they equate a Comdex ranking of "50" with a failing grade.

7 K.E.Y. questions

My first book, "*Simple LTC Solution: How to Protect Your Life's Savings with a Long-Term Care Partnership Program,*" focused on seven "K.E.Y." questions. "K.E.Y." stands for:

Knowledge **E**mpowers **Y**ou

These "K.E.Y." questions can help you better understand what kind of product an "A-to-Z" is trying to sell you. These questions will help you cut through all the jargon and help you determine which policies to reject and which policies to consider seriously.

K.E.Y. Question #1:
Which type of policy are you quoting for me?
    1. Traditional long-term care insurance,
    2. Long-term care partnership policy,
    3. Recovery policy,
    4. Life insurance with some type of rider
    5. An annuity with some type of rider,
    6. (or something else)?

K.E.Y. Question #2:
Within the last two* years, have you taken the training required to sell long-term care partnership policies? ** If they answer "no", that

means they do not sell the type of long-term care coverage that is the best type of policy for most people.

*Connecticut, Indiana, and New York do not require ongoing training. These three states require long-term care partnership training to be taken only once.

**Four states do not require any special training to sell long-term care insurance: Alaska, Hawaii, Mississippi, and Vermont. At the time of publication, these four states are the only states that have not yet enacted some type of "Long-Term Care Partnership Program."

K.E.Y. Question #3:
If I need to make a claim and use this policy in the very first year I own it, what is the maximum amount it will pay for each month I need care?

K.E.Y. Question #4:
If I need to use this policy in the future, what is the maximum amount it will pay for each month I need care 5 years from now? 15 years from now? 25 years from now? 35 years from now?

Are these amounts guaranteed, or are they just projections?

K.E.Y. Question #5:
How much is this policy's "Lifetime Benefit"?
Does the "Lifetime Benefit" grow over time?
If the "Lifetime Benefit" grows over time, how much will it be 5 years from now? 15 years from now? 25 years from now? 35 years from now?

Are these amounts guaranteed, or are they just projections?

K.E.Y. Question #6:
If the benefits increase, will the premium also increase?

K.E.Y. Question #7:

If an "A-to-Z" is trying to sell you a life insurance policy with some kind of rider, you MUST ask this question: "What is the premium I must pay to guarantee that this policy stays in-force until at least my 100th birthday?" Then, ask them to show you the page of the illustration with the "guaranteed premium" and the "guaranteed death benefit through age 100".

Chapter 8
What has Washington State wrought?

What is the WA Cares Fund?

The WA Cares Fund (formerly known as the "Washington Long-Term Care Trust Act") is the first government-run, long-term care insurance program. It was signed into law by Governor Inslee in 2019.

The program is funded through a payroll deduction of 58 cents for every $100 of W-2 income (i.e., .58%). The first payroll deductions began in July 2023. The first benefits will be paid to eligible participants beginning July 2026.

The program's benefit is $36,500, periodically adjusted for inflation. $36,500 is the maximum amount of benefit payable for life, <u>not</u> per year. The program is not intended to cover the full cost of care but to provide a small amount of benefits to decrease dependence upon Medicaid.

The program is not universal. It does not cover:
- those who are already retired,
- those who are already disabled and can't work or
- stay-at-home parents

What Washington state did right (& wrong)

The state of Washington did a lot of things right when they created this program. The program has a modest payroll deduction suitable for the modest amount of benefits.

The program is actuarially sound. Most workers will pay into the fund for 10 years before they will be able to qualify for benefits. The program does not cover those who are already retired.

Benefits are flexible, allowing many different care settings as well as many different care providers (even family members in certain cases).

The program provides first-dollar benefits. In other words, other than the time required to file a claim, no deductible must be paid before receiving the benefits.

After its initial passage, the legislators improved the law in 2020, 2021, and 2022 (based on feedback from constituents and stakeholders).

They allowed citizens who already owned private long-term care insurance a one-time opt-out from the program.

The state of Washington did only one thing wrong. They underestimated how many people would buy private long-term care insurance to opt-out of the program (and avoid the payroll deduction). Initially, the actuaries estimated that 105,000 workers would buy private long-term care insurance and opt-out of the program. Over 480,000 of the highest-paid workers in the state bought private long-term care insurance and opted out of the program.

For highly compensated workers who were healthy enough, a small, private long-term care insurance policy was a better deal than paying the state .58% of W-2 earnings.

LONG-TERM CARE INSURANCE NOW!

2 ways the WA Cares Fund and private LTCi are nearly identical

The WA Cares Fund and private long-term care insurance are nearly identical in two of the most important ways:

#1: Comprehensive benefits
Both the WA Cares Fund and private long-term care insurance policies offer comprehensive benefits: care at home, home modifications, adult day care, care in assisted-living facilities, and nursing home care.

About 60% of private long-term care insurance claims start and/or end at home. That is what happened with my mother-in-law. Her first couple months of care were at home. She then transitioned to an assisted-living facility for a few years. She then moved into our home after COVID hit.

Her long-term care insurance policy paid for a home health aide while she lived with us. Her policy also paid to have the bathroom modified with a walk-in shower, as well as several grab bars throughout the house. The WA Cares Fund can also pay for similar home modifications.

#2: Adequate reserves to pay all future claims
Both the WA Cares Fund and private long-term care insurance companies MUST set aside adequate reserves to pay all future claims.

There has been a lot of political rhetoric about the "solvency of the WA Cares Fund." The law that created the WA Cares Fund requires that the fund be solvent. If necessary, the Trustees must lower the benefits in the future to keep the fund solvent.

Private long-term care insurance companies also must fully fund their reserves to pay all future claims. Private long-term care insurance companies canNOT lower policyholders' benefits if their claims projections are much higher than originally expected. Private long-term care insurance companies have a limited right to request a premium increase for all policyholders with similar policies if their claims projections become much higher than originally expected.

6 ways the WA Cares Fund is better than private long-term care insurance

The WA Cares Fund is better than private long-term care insurance in 6 ways:

#1: No underwriting
The hardest part of private long-term care insurance is the underwriting. You canNOT buy private long-term care insurance just because you want to buy it. You must be healthy enough to qualify. The biggest advantage of the WA Cares Fund is that there is no medical underwriting. Everyone employed in the state of Washington can contribute to the program.

#2: No premiums when retired (or unemployed)
Another excellent feature of the WA Cares Fund is that you only pay the premiums while you are working. When you retire, you no longer pay any premiums. If you are unemployed, you also do not have to pay premiums. You only pay the premium when you are working. With most private long-term care insurance policies, the premiums must be paid as long as you live, even after you retire. There are a few private long-term care insurance policies where you only need to pay premiums for a set number of years (e.g., 10 years).

#3: Family caregivers
Another important feature of the WA Cares Fund is that it can pay the benefits to a family member who is caring for you. Most private long-term care insurance policies will NOT pay a family member to care for you.

#4: No daily benefit
An incredibly unique feature of the WA Cares Fund is that there is no daily benefit, only a lifetime benefit. Every private long-term care

insurance policy has a "daily benefit" or a "monthly benefit," as well as a "lifetime benefit."

The "daily benefit" is the most the policy will pay for each day you receive care.

The "monthly benefit" is similar. It is the most the policy will pay for each month that you need care.

The "lifetime benefit" is the most the policy will pay in benefits over your lifetime.

The WA Cares Fund has a "lifetime benefit" of $36,500 (adjusted for inflation). However, the WA Cares Fund has no "daily benefit" nor a "monthly benefit."

For example, if your care costs $100 per day, the WA Cares Fund would pay the $100 per day for 365 days. ($36,500 divided by $100 = 365 days).

However, if you need more than $100 per day of care, for example, if you need care that costs $365 per day, the WA Cares Fund would pay the $365 per day, and it would stop paying after 100 days.

($36,500 lifetime benefit divided by $365 per day = 100 days)

With private long-term care insurance, if your daily benefit is $200, it will not pay any more than that for each day of care. You must pay any costs you incur that are over the daily benefit. That is why, when purchasing a private long-term care insurance policy, one of the most important decisions you need to make is how much of a daily (or monthly) benefit you want your policy to have.

#5: Unisex rates
Another distinctive feature of the WA Cares Fund is that the payroll deduction of .58% is the same regardless of gender. Most, but not all,

private long-term care insurance policies charge different rates based on gender. Men usually pay less for private long-term care insurance than women pay because men are more likely to die suddenly without needing care. Women tend to live longer and are more likely to need care than men.

#6: Rates are the same regardless of age:
Lastly, the WA Cares Fund does not charge premiums based on age. Every employed person in the state pays the same rate regardless of their age. That rate is 58 cents for every $100 of W-2 earnings.

Private long-term care insurance policies determine your premium based on the age you are when you apply for your policy. The younger you are when you apply for a private long-term care insurance policy, the lower your premium. The older you are when you apply for a policy, the higher your premium will be.

9 Ways Private Long-Term Care Insurance is BETTER than the WA Cares Fund

#1: Is inflation protection guaranteed?

<u>WA Cares:</u>
No.
The WA Cares Fund does not guarantee that benefits will grow every year. One of the most important things to consider when planning for long-term care is inflation. The cost of care is increasing primarily due to labor shortages.
The WA Cares Fund will increase the Fund's benefits periodically based on the increase in the cost of living in the state of Washington. However, the increases in the benefits are not guaranteed. In fact, the law requires that the increases only be implemented if the trust is adequately funded. The growth in the WA Cares Fund benefits is at the discretion of the trustees. It's not guaranteed.

Private LTC Insurance:
Yes.
Private long-term care insurance has inflation protection that is fully guaranteed. When you buy a long-term care insurance policy, you choose how much inflation protection you want. Every year, your policy benefits will grow by that amount. If, for example, you choose a 3% compound inflation protection, your benefits will grow EVERY YEAR by exactly 3% compounding. With nearly every policy sold today, the growth in the benefits each year does NOT make the premium go up each year. The 3% compounded growth is built into the premium from the start. The growth in the benefits is guaranteed every year, even while you are on claim and receiving benefits from the policy.

#2: WILL MY PREMIUMS GO UP?

WA Cares:
Yes.
The WA Cares Fund has, essentially, built-in premium increases. Every time someone gets a pay raise, the amount they pay into the WA Cares Fund goes up. For example, someone making $100,000 per year pays $580 into the WA Cares Fund each year. If that person gets a $50,000 bonus one year, the amount they would have to pay into WA Cares that year would be $870 ($150,000 x .58% = $870). Every time they get a pay raise or a bonus, the amount they have to pay into the Fund goes up, but the amount of benefits they can get from the program stays the same.

Private LTC Insurance:
Maybe.
Private long-term care insurance policies purchased in the state of Washington have very strict rate increase regulations. All long-term care insurance policies purchased in Washington since 2008 must comply with Washington state's "Rate Stability Regulation".

The "Rate Stability Regulation" in Washington, forces the insurance companies to lower their profits if they seek a rate increase. It also forbids the insurance companies from including normal profit margins in the rate increase itself. By removing the profit incentive from rate increases this regulation is helping to curb rate increases on newer long-term care insurance policies purchased in Washington since 2008.

#3: Does it protect my assets from Medicaid?

WA Cares:
No.
The WA Cares Fund does not protect your assets from Medicaid. If you use up all $36,500 of benefits from the WA Cares Fund, you then have to use your savings and/or income to pay for your care. Once you've spent your savings down to $2,000, you can apply for Medicaid-funded long-term care.

Private LTC Insurance:
Yes.
Private long-term care insurance policies can protect your assets from Medicaid even if you exhaust the benefits in your long-term care insurance policy. These special policies are called "Long-Term Care Partnership" policies.

If, for example, your private long-term care insurance policy has $300,000 of benefits and you use up all of the benefits, you can apply for Medicaid and you can keep $302,000 of savings and still be able to qualify for Medicaid-funded long-term care. This is called "Dollar for Dollar" Asset Protection. Every dollar you receive in benefits from your policy allows you to protect one dollar from Medicaid.

#4: How long does it take to be fully vested?

WA Cares:
10 years to fully vest.

You must contribute to the WA Cares Fund for 10 years before you are fully vested. You won't stop contributing after 10 years. You continue to contribute to the program for as long as you earn W-2 income. People born before 1968 can be partially vested. Each year that they contribute to the WA Cares Fund, they will be 10% vested.

Private LTC Insurance:
Immediate vesting.
Private long-term care insurance policies do not have any "vesting period". Once you have applied, have been approved, and have paid your first premium, you are fully vested.

#5: CAN I EVER GET A REFUND OF THE PREMIUMS I'VE PAID?

WA Cares:
No.
If you never need long-term care, WA Cares will not give you back any of the premiums you paid into the Fund.

Private LTC Insurance:
Yes.
Some private long-term care insurance policies offer a "return of premium" feature. If the policyholder passes away without using the policy benefits, 100% of the premiums are refunded to the heir(s). If the policyholder needs some care, the amount refunded is usually the sum of premiums paid minus the amount of claims received from the policy.

#6: CAN I CUSTOMIZE MY BENEFITS?

WA Cares:
No.
Everyone in the WA Cares Fund has the same amount of benefits ($36,500, adjusted for inflation) and the same inflation protection. The inflation protection will fluctuate every couple of years or so.

Private LTC Insurance:
Yes.
This is probably the biggest advantage of private long-term care insurance. There are hundreds of ways to tailor a private long-term care insurance policy to fit your needs, goals, and budget. With private long-term care insurance policies today, you can choose a daily maximum as low as $100 to as high as $500, inflation protection as low as 1% compound to as high as 5% compound, and a lifetime maximum as low as $36,500 to as high as $1.4 million. The richer the benefits you choose, the higher the policy's premium. The lower the benefits you choose, the lower the policy's premium.

#7: IS THE PREMIUM TAX-DEDUCTIBLE?

WA Cares:
No.
The WA Cares Fund is NOT tax-deductible. The deduction comes out of each paycheck AFTER taxes. If you're in a 28% federal income tax bracket, the .58% payroll deduction is effectively costing you .74%.

Private LTC Insurance:
Yes.
Private long-term care insurance premiums are tax-deductible, AND the benefits are 100% tax-free for reimbursement policies. (In very rare cases, some benefits paid from a "cash indemnity" policy may be taxable.)

#8: IF I USE UP ALL MY BENEFITS AND FULLY RECOVER, CAN I USE THE BENEFITS AGAIN IF I NEED CARE AGAIN IN THE FUTURE?

WA Cares:
No.
With the WA Cares Fund, once you use up the $36,500 (adjusted for inflation), you never get any more benefits, even if you fully recover and start to work again.

Private LTC Insurance:

Yes.

Some private long-term care insurance policies have what is called a "Restoration of Benefits" feature. That means that if you recover, your benefits can be restored, and you can use the full amount of benefits more than once. For example, suppose you buy a private long-term care insurance policy with $150,000 of benefits. Suppose you need care and you use up all those benefits. If you fully recover, the benefits you received from the policy can be put back into the policy. That $150,000 of benefits could end up being $300,000 of benefits if you need to use the policy more than once.

#9: Can my benefits be changed without my consent?

WA Cares:

The WA Cares Fund Trustees can (and are legally required to) lower the benefits if needed in order to keep the program solvent. Washington state legislators can also pass new laws to change the program's benefits anytime in the future.

Private LTC insurance:

Once you buy a private long-term care insurance policy, the insurance company canNOT change the benefits of the policy. Every week, I read someone posting on the internet that "long-term care insurance companies can lower benefits as policyholders age." That's 100% false. Once you buy a private long-term care insurance policy, the insurance company canNOT lower the benefits. YOU can choose to lower your benefits at any time if you want to, but the insurance company canNOT lower your benefits.

Thank you for reading my book!

If you have any questions about anything I've written in this book, please email me directly at Scott@LTCShop.com.

I'll reply as quickly as I can.

If you've found this book helpful, please let others know. It would be especially helpful if you left a review on Amazon.com.

Thanks!

About the Author

Scott A. Olson, CLTC, is a highly regarded expert in long-term care planning with over 25 years of experience. In 1999, he was one of the first insurance professionals to earn the Certified in Long-Term Care designation. He is licensed to sell long-term care insurance in all 50 states and is a co-founder of LTCShop.com. As a long-term care insurance specialist, he provides tailored solutions emphasizing clarity and personalized strategies. Scott's first book, "Simple LTC Solution: How to Protect Your Life Savings with a Long-Term Care Partnership Policy" has thousands of copies in print. Scott was born and raised in New Jersey and attended Rutgers University. He began his insurance career in the mid-eighties. Scott then switched gears and spent four years doing charitable work in the Caribbean. In 1995 he re-entered the insurance industry focusing exclusively on long-term care insurance. Scott and his wife, Carolyn, have four sons, and they live in San Marcos, Texas.

www.ingramcontent.com/pod-product-compliance
Lightning Source LLC
Chambersburg PA
CBHW030945180526
45163CB00002B/707